T0065691

ROMANS
THE GOSPEL OF GRACE

MARC D. SIMON

WESTBOW
PRESS®
A DIVISION OF THOMAS NELSON
& ZONDERVAN

WestBow Press books may be ordered through booksellers or by contacting:

WestBow Press
A Division of Thomas Nelson & Zondervan
1663 Liberty Drive
Bloomington, IN 47403
www.westbowpress.com
844-714-3454

ISBN: 978-1-6642-8524-8 (sc)
ISBN: 978-1-6642-8526-2 (hc)
ISBN: 978-1-6642-8525-5 (e)

Library of Congress Control Number: 2022922310

Print information available on the last page.

WestBow Press rev. date: 12/15/2022

CONTENTS

INTRODUCTION

THE LETTERS WRITTEN BY PAUL are among the earliest writings we possess from the New Testament era.[1] They were sent to various churches and people by Paul as a form of pastoral correspondence years before many of the New Testament writings existed in their present forms. The letter which he sends to Rome is perhaps the most exhaustive witness to Paul's theology and teaching left by Paul himself. So highly was the letter regarded by leaders of the reformation that Luther famously wrote:

> This Epistle is really the chief part of the New Testament and the very purest Gospel, and is worthy not only that every Christian should know it word for word, by heart, but occupy himself with it every day, as the daily bread of the soul.[2]

Romans remains one of the most studied (and debated) books in the entire Bible and has been called by some the Cathedral of the Christian faith itself.

The Occasion and Purpose of the Letter

Paul likely composed Romans from Cenchreae, a port-city near Corinth, between AD 56–57. He dictated the letter to a man named Tertius (cf. 16:22),[3] and entrusted its deliverance to a wealthy deaconess named Phoebe (cf. 16:1–2).

---

[1] Hays, R. B., *Echoes of Scripture in the Letters of Paul* (1993)

[2] Luther, M., "Preface to the Epistle to the Romans" (1522)

[3] According to tradition, Tertius later became the Bishop of Iconium.

After nearly ten years in the region, Paul planned to deliver a large offering from the assemblies in the eastern Mediterranean to Jerusalem. From there he planned to travel to Rome, which he hoped to use as a base of operations for his missionary work in the west, just as Antioch had served as his primary base in the east. The letter he sends ahead of his arrival is a literary and theological triumph, shaped by his Christological reading of the Hebrew Scriptures, as well as his pastoral concern for the believers in Rome.

The Major Theme of the Letter

Romans is rooted in Paul's conviction that Christ died for our sins according to the Scriptures (1 Cor. 15:3-4), and that his resurrection signaled the beginning of the new creation promised by God. The major theme of the letter, which factors in every chapter, is outlined in Romans 1:16-17.

> I am not ashamed of the gospel of Christ. It is the power
> of God to salvation for all those who believe–beginning
> with the Jew, but also the Greek. In it the righteousness
> of God is revealed from faith to faith, even as it is written:
> the just shall live by faith.

In short, the gospel is the revelation of God's righteousness, meaning his covenant faithfulness and justice, as well as his unswerving commitment to creation. What Paul expounds in Romans is not an improvised system of theology or teaching, but the gospel itself, meaning the good news of Israel's Messiah, Jesus the Christ, as Paul has received and understood it directly from Jesus himself.

1

SHARING THE GOSPEL

Romans 1:1–17

[1] Paul, a servant of Jesus Christ, called as an apostle, and set apart by God for the gospel [2] promised through his prophets in the holy scriptures. [3] The gospel is about his son, who was descended from David according to the flesh; [4] and declared the Son of God in power according to the Spirit of holiness at his resurrection from the dead. He is Jesus Christ, our Lord! [5] By him we have received the grace of apostleship, calling every nation to the obedience of faith in his name, [6] among whom you also have been called. [7] I am writing to all of you in Rome who are loved of God, and called and set apart as his own. May the grace and peace of our God and Father, and our Lord Jesus Christ be with you.

[8] Let me begin by saying that I thank God through Jesus Christ for all of you. People all over the world are talking about your faith. [9] God is my witness, who I serve in my spirit through the gospel of his son, that I have held you [10] in my prayers; asking that by his will I might finally see you. [11] For I have longed to see you in person and to impart something of benefit to you; [12] and to also be uplifted by our shared faith as well. [13] I don't want you to be unaware that I often made plans to visit you in the past but was hindered. My hope is that I might now bear some fruit among you, just as I have among other nations.

[14] For I am obligated to both Greeks and non-Greeks—those who are wise and those who are unwise, [15] and am ready to proclaim the gospel among you in Rome.

[16] You see, I am not ashamed of the gospel of Christ. It is the power of God to salvation for all those who believe—beginning with the Jew, but also the Greek. [17]

In it the righteousness of God is revealed from faith to faith, even as it is written: the just shall live by faith,

1. Paul, a servant of Jesus Christ, called as an apostle, and set apart by God for the gospel...

Paul begins his letter by introducing himself as a *servant*, an *apostle*, and as one *set apart*. Each of these terms expresses a unique aspect of his relationship with Jesus. As a servant, he was obedient. As an apostle, he exercised authority. And as one who had been set apart his life was no longer his own, but God's.[4]

The Greek word translated "servant" denotes one who was bound to another as a slave. Paul had willingly followed the pattern of Jesus, who emptied himself during his earthly life as well and lived in this world as a servant to others (cf. Phil. 2:7).

That Paul was called as an apostle means that he had not taken the title for himself but had been called to it by God. He makes this point even clearer in Galatians when he writes that his apostleship was neither from men, nor through man, but from God the Father and Jesus Christ (Gal. 1:1).

Luther believed that Paul was set apart by God through the word of the Holy Spirit in Antioch ("Set apart for me Barnabas and Saul")[5] as well as God's election of Paul before his birth.[6]

The gospel ("good news") wasn't simply a message about our salvation but was the proclamation that a physical descendant of David had been raised from death by God as the world's rightful king.

> Remember that Jesus Christ, a descendant of David, was raised from the dead according to my gospel. (2 Tim. 2:8)

---

[4] Cf. Galatians 1:15, where Paul states that he was divinely set apart by God before his birth.

[5] Acts 13:2

[6] Galatians 1:15; cf. Isa. 49:1; Jer. 1:5

For Paul, the resurrection was the witness of God's faithfulness in Jesus, through whom the life of the coming age had now been unveiled.

It is the Christian belief in a lord other than Caesar that many in Rome found troubling, seeing as the declaration of the church ("Jesus is Lord") both mirrored and contested that of Rome itself ("Caesar is Lord"). When added to Paul's practice of asking Roman citizens to financially support efforts in Jerusalem (cf. 1 Cor. 16:1–2)[7] one can easily see why some felt his work might be potentially dangerous, or subversive.

3. The gospel is about his son, who was descended from David...

It was not a new philosophy or religion that Paul had been called to announce to the world, but a person – *Jesus Christ the son of David* – through whom the God of Israel had now entered creation.

It is highly probable that Paul is using the word "Lord" (kurios) to infer both the divine nature of Christ and his royal status as David's heir. The word *kurios* was the common way of translating Yahweh (the Hebrew name for the covenant God of Israel), as well as Adonai (the Hebrew word for "lord") into Greek.

4. Declared the Son of God in power...

By "declared the Son of God in power," Paul is not saying that Jesus became God's Son at the resurrection, but asserting that his Sonship was uniquely demonstrated by this event.

The designation "Son of God" properly names one aspect of the preexisting relationship within God between the Father and the Son, and it also denotes the Messianic hopes of Israel, for whom the coming Davidic king was also the Son of God, cf. "You are my son, today I have begotten you" (Psalm 2:7); "...and he will be my son" (2 Sam. 7:14).

---

[7] Cf. *"For if non-Jews have shared in the spiritual blessings of the Jews, they ought to be of service to them in their material blessings"* (Rom. 15:27).

5. The grace of apostleship...

By linking grace to apostleship, Paul likely means "the grace of being called as an apostle." It was by grace, and not any merit of their own, that men were called to the apostolic office by God.

Obedience of faith in his name...

By "obedience of faith," Paul is not referring to something that we do or bring about in our own strength. In fact, faith itself is not a "doing" at all, but the first fruit of the Spirit's influence in our lives. As Paul says elsewhere, it is God, working through the Spirit, who initiates and enables both our faith and its confession (cf. 1 Cor. 12:3).

7. Grace and peace...

The words *grace* and *peace* combine Greek and Hebrew greetings in a way that highlights both the gift of God (cf. Eph. 2:8; Rom. 6:23) and the well-being of those who receive it in faith.

8. I thank God through Jesus Christ for all of you...

Just as Paul had received God's calling through the mediation of Jesus (cf. v. 5), it is through Jesus that he now offers his thanks back to God.

> There is one God and one mediator between God and men, the man Jesus Christ. (1 Timothy 2:5)

11. And to impart something of benefit to you...

The words "to impart something of benefit" literally mean to give a share of something useful. Paul is not implying that he distributes spiritual gifts to others but that he shares with them the grace and gifting that God has shared with him.

Paul never names the exact hindrance that had prevented him from visiting Rome in the past. It is a fact of history that Claudius (AD 41–54) demanded the expulsion of Jews from Rome during the early years of Paul's ministry. According to the Roman historian Suetonius, the reason for the expulsion was that the Jews had created disturbances in Rome because of a figure named Chrestus, which may be a Latinism for Christ.

Either way, the expulsion is briefly referred to in Acts 18:2, where Aquila and Priscilla are said to have come to Corinth from Italy, "because Claudius had ordered all of the Jews to leave Rome." It is widely speculated that it was the expulsion of Jews from Rome that hindered Paul from entering the city at an earlier date. Of this point, however, we cannot be certain.

16. I am not ashamed of the gospel of Christ.

For Paul, the good news was not a proclamation about a new religion or belief, but a proclamation about a person–*Jesus of Nazareth,* the earthly descendant of David.

According to Paul, when the good news about Jesus is announced to others, God demonstrates his power towards those who have faith by justifying them in the present and delivering them from wrath in the future (cf. Rom. 2:5; 1 Thess. 1:10).

The power of God to salvation for all those who believe.

The salvation that Paul speaks of is not an escape from the present world but our deliverance from the death that has infected it. Fundamental to his teaching is the conviction that those who are being saved are not yet perfected in the present world but being gradually transformed from one state of glory to another (cf. 2 Cor. 3:18). We are thence saved by grace, experienced through both our present faith and future hope.

There are two additional points from the above verse that should be noted. Firstly, the gospel is only effective (meaning "unto salvation") in those who receive it in faith. And secondly, faith is the only condition given for its reception.

17. The righteousness of God.

The exact sense that Paul intends God's "righteousness" in the present verse has been debated at length. The argument is whether Paul is referring to the "justness" of God himself, in which case it is the righteousness "of God,"[8] or the status that God confers on man in salvation, in which case it is the righteousness "from God." Either way, early believers understood this righteousness to mean that God was both just and the justifier of those who trust in him.

The just shall live by faith.

Paul ends this section with a quotation from Habakkuk 2:4, which literally means that the just live, or experience life, by faith. In the ancient mind, being just meant living in fidelity towards God. What Paul is arguing is that being just is really a matter of the faith we have in Christ. Those who are made righteous by this faith, will live by this same faith in the present world.

This of course, is what Habakkuk was saying to the Jews in Babylonian exile 600 years before Paul. In the same way as the exiles in Babylon were to live by their faith in God, Paul's readers in Rome were to now live by their faith in Jesus, through whom God was now present among them as well.

---

[8] cf. "the righteous activity of God" (Jewett); "God's salvation-creating power" (Kasemann); "God's saving righteousness" (Schreiner); "the saving activity of God" (Talbert); "His covenant faithfulness" (Dunn); "his dynamic fidelity to his covenant promises" (Dumbrell).

II

SIN AND JUDGMENT

Romans 1:18–2:16

[18] God's anger is now being revealed from heaven against ungodliness and injustice in those who have unrightly suppressed the truth. [19] For what can be known about God is evident even to them, for God himself has made it known. [20] We even see his eternal power and divine nature displayed in creation. And though we do not see them directly, they are discerned in the things that are created, so that men are without excuse. [21] For though they witness God in creation, they neither honor him, nor give thanks. Instead, they have given themselves over to useless thinking and the darkening of their hearts. [22] Declaring themselves wise, they became fools, [23] exchanging God's eternal glory for graven images shaped like men, birds, animals, and even reptiles.

[24] For this reason God gave them over to what they wanted, seeing as they dishonored themselves, [25] and traded God's truth for the lie. In doing so, they have given more honor to created things then to God himself, who alone is eternally blessed. Amen.

[26] Because of this, God gave them over to what they wanted, until even their women gave up their natural relations with men in exchange for what is unnatural. [27] The men likewise turned away from their natural relations with women and burned in their desire for one another. Men committing shameful acts with men and receiving in themselves a just recompence for their error.

[28] To the same extent that they refused to acknowledge him; God gave them over to the things they wanted. [29] As a result they were filled with injustice, wickedness and greed, evil and envious thoughts, murder, strife and deceit, slanders. They

became gossipers, [30] whisperers, haters of God; defiant, self-important, boasters, inventors of evil, disobedient even to parents; [31] unwise, unfaithful, and unfeeling. [32] Knowing that God has said that such things are worthy of death, they not only do them, but encourage others who do them as well.

2 Now you may rightly judge such people as being evil, but you who are judging are in many ways as evil as them, and yet without excuse. In judging them you are condemning your own selves, because you are judging them while being guilty of the same sins. [2] Now we know that God's judgment is unbiased and based on truth. [3] Do you think that by judging others while also being in sin that you will escape the judgment that comes from God?

[4] Have you disregarded his goodness and forbearing patience, not knowing that his goodness is what draws you to repentance? [5] Because you have hardened your hearts and refuse to repent, you are laying up for yourselves wrath on the day of God's righteous judgment, [6] when God himself renders to every soul according to its work.

[7] To those who patiently do what is good, seeking glory, honor, and immortality, the life of the coming age. [8] But for those who live for themselves in rebellion against truth and righteousness, there will be wrath and indignation. [9] Tribulation and despair await those who traffic in evil—beginning with the Jew, but also the Greek. [10] But glory, honor and peace await those who labor in good—beginning with the Jew, but also the Greek. [11] For there is no partiality in such matters with God.

[12] Whoever sins outside of the law, will perish outside of the law, and whoever sins while knowing the law, will be judged by the law. [13] For hearing the law alone will not make us right with God, but doing what the law says is what he declares right.

[14] So when Gentiles who have never heard the law act in agreement with the law they are proving that the law itself is already operating within them. [15] Their very actions are a proof [16] and their conscience a witness as well, for their own thoughts will either accuse or defend them on the day God judges the hidden things of men through Christ Jesus. And this is what I announce in the gospel.

---

18. God's anger is now being revealed...

From the human vantage God appears to be acting in anger when he punishes sin. Calvin argued however, that Paul was not simply attributing the emotion of anger to God but appealing to the perception of those punished. God's wrath, he wrote, was not the self-regarding passion of one slighted, but the just answer of Absolute Holiness to sin.

Ungodliness and injustice...

Paul here identifies ungodliness and injustice as the proper objects of God's anger. While the former implies impiety towards God himself, the latter infers the violation of rights among human beings.

19. What can be known about God is evident...

Paul here lays the foundation for what we today call natural revelation, which affirms that God is revealed in creation itself, as well as the human conscience. For this reason, Hebrews calls the world a mirrored representation of the invisible, and David, in the psalms, calls the visible heavens a revelation of invisible glory.

> The heavens proclaim his glory, and the skies his workmanship. Day after day they speak, and night after night they reveal knowledge. Yet their speech is without sound or word, and their voice unheard. Still, their message goes out to all the earth and their words to all the world. (Psalm 19:1–4)

20. They are discerned in the things that are created...

For Paul, God's power and deity were discernable in the things that were made by God himself. On contemplating even simple things in creation, man ought to grasp enough of God himself to keep him from idolatry and materialism. We should note that Paul's words have as much relevance for those today who have made money, status, or sex their "god" as for those who once fashioned "gods" out of wood and stone.

21. They witness God in creation...

Paul states that God has given every person the means of discerning him in creation. None are exempt because God has plainly revealed himself through things made.

22. They became fools...

The fool, according to David, is the one who says, "there is no God."[9] In the same manner, Paul states that those who failed to acknowledge God became fools, meaning morally and spiritually dull, and not simply deficient in intelligence or reasoning. Spiritually speaking, moral corruption correlates to a type of atheism.

23. Exchanging God's eternal glory...

While Israel had been guilty of exchanging the worship of the true God for the image of a calf, Paul attributes this same sin to every nation under heaven, and not simply the Jews. In his idolatry man worships things placed beneath him in creation, taking things from the earth and calling them "gods."

24. God gave them over...

Paul uses this term three separate times in Romans to describe God's judgment of sin (vv. 24, 26, 28). In this context God's wrath is simply the removal of his restraint, leaving men to their desire and its consequence. What some have viewed as God's punishment in their lives is often simply the consequence of being given over to their sin. In this same way Paul tells his Corinthian readers to "deliver" the unrepentant man to Satan (1 Cor. 5:5), which is his way of saying that if he will not repent of his sin, then at some point he should be given up to it.

25. [they] traded God's truth for the lie.

The expression in Greek, tēn alētheian tou theou, literally denotes the singular and definite truth of God, which Paul contrasts with the singular and definite lie (tō pseúdei), which is untruth in an absolute sense.

---

[9] Psalm 14:1 (KJV)

26. Their women gave up their natural relations with men in exchange for what is unnatural.

While the Hebrew scriptures prohibited homosexuality (cf. Lev. 18:22), Paul makes no mention of the Mosaic standard here, nor does he seek to impose it onto his non-Jewish readers. Rather, he speaks of the law of nature itself and classifies sexual acts as those that are either in accord with nature or contrary to it.

27. A just recompense for their error.

The phrase "just recompense for their error" is not an indicator of a special punishment meted out for homosexuality, but an affirmation that God is just in recompensing it when he does. While the Old Testament does not take up the specifics of sexual acts between men and women, it does clearly state who one should or should not engage in sexual acts with (see Lev. 18:6–23).

28. To the same extent that they refused to acknowledge him...

Paul is not simply telling his readers why God gave some over to a base mind but emphasizing that God was completely just or fair in the extent to which he did. In other words, the degree to which God gave them over corresponded exactly to the degree to which they themselves had already turned away.

29–31. As a result, they were filled with injustice, wickedness...

These verses make up the longest list of this kind found in the New Testament and show the personal and social evils that arise when men are given over to sin. Similar lists can be found in Matt. 15:19; 1 Cor. 6:9–10; Gal. 5:19–21; Eph. 4:31; Col. 3:5; 1 Tim. 1:9–10; and 2 Tim. 3:2–5.

2. God's judgment is unbiased and based on truth.

Having sufficiently addressed man's outward sin, Paul now contends with his hidden self-righteousness. The repetition of the words *beginning with the Jew, but equally to the Greek*[10] emphasize the point that while the Jew would be the first to experience judgment, he was also the first to receive grace.

4. His goodness is what draws you to repentance.

Though repentance factors heavily in the synoptic gospels and Acts,[11] the present verse is the only place in Romans where Paul explicitly uses the term.

6. God himself renders to every soul according to its work.

"Judgment," Tertullian wrote, "has been ordained by God according to the merits of every man" (cf. Job 34:10–11; Jer. 17:10; Matt.16:27; 1 Cor. 3:8; 2 Cor. 5:10; and Rom. 14:12).

7. To those who patiently do what is good...

Some have mistakenly read verse 7 as if Paul were affirming that salvation ensues from our own patient doing of what is good (works!). This is an error for multiple reasons. First, as Paul soon clarifies, all people, without exception, sin.[12] Second, what Paul is addressing here is the basis of God's judgment, not his salvation.[13] When read in its context (vv. 7–11), God's impartiality as judge is the proper subject of these verses, and not the basis upon which he saves human beings, which Paul wont explicitly spell out until 3:21.

The life of the coming age.

Throughout his letters Paul uses the phrase "life of the coming age" as a referent for the life experienced in the resurrection or world to come. Paul argues that to share in the life of the coming age is to also share in the life of its Lord, Jesus Christ, who is eternal.

---

[10] see 2:9 and 10

[11] See: Matt. 3:2, 4:17; Mk. 1:15, 6:12; Lk. 13:3; Acts 2:38, 3:19. **Note:** the word *"repentance"* does not appear at all in any of John's writings, except for Revelation.

[12] Cf. Romans 3:23

[13] Cf. Romans 2:5–6

11. There is no partiality in such matters with God.

Just as God makes the sun rise and set on the just and the unjust alike, so the followers of Jesus were to now extend themselves to both friend and enemy alike without partiality.

13–14. Hearing the law...doing what the law says.

Paul here distinguishes between those who have heard the law and those who do the law, with the latter being just before God. But what does it mean to do the law, and is Paul suggesting that we are made righteous by doing things? We will return to this question shortly.

For now, what Paul seems to be indicating is that it was possible, at least hypothetically, for those who did not possess the written law to still "do the law" based upon the law being written in their hearts. This may also be an allusion to the New Covenant promise of Jeremiah 31:33.

> And this is the covenant that I will make with the house of Israel after those days, declares the LORD: I myself will set my law within them, and write it upon their hearts.

15–16. Their very actions are a proof and their conscience a witness as well.

For Paul, the word conscience implies a kind of knower within each of us which examines and critiques our own thoughts and behaviors. Through a healthy conscience we witness our own thoughts and behaviors and judge them accordingly.

> If we would judge ourselves rightly, we would not come under the judgment of others. (1 Cor. 11:31)

Jack Hayford, in his Bible Handbook (1995), more fully defines our conscience as our own awareness of conforming to, or departing from God's standard, resulting in either self-approval or self-condemnation.

III

BOASTING IN GOD

Romans 2:17–3:8

[17] Now to the one who calls himself a Jew. You have relied on the law and made your boast in God. [18] You have known his will and followed a more excellent way, being guided by the law itself. [19] You have even led the blind and given light to those in darkness, [20] and instructed fools and infants through your knowledge of the law.

[21] Yes, you have busied yourselves teaching others, but have you been teaching yourselves? You declare that men should not steal, but is their stealing among you? [22] You speak against adultery, but do you engage in it? You have spoken against idols, but do you partake of things offered in their temples? [23] Though you boast in the law, you have dishonored God by breaking it! [24] His very name is blasphemed among the nations because of you, just as it is written.

[25] Now circumcision is profitable if you keep the rest of the law as well; but if you break the law, are you really any different from those who are uncircumcised? [26] And if those who are uncircumcised fulfill the law, are they really any different from those who are physically circumcised? [27] Will not the uncircumcised who uphold the law judge those who break it despite being physically circumcised and having the commandments?

[28] For one is not made a Jew through outward means, nor is real circumcision a matter of the flesh. [29] But the Jew is one inwardly; and their circumcision a matter of the heart and the spirit, not the letter; whose praise is from God, and not from men.

3 Then what more does the Jew have than others? Is there any benefit in his circumcision? ² Yes, in every way, seeing as it was the Jew who was entrusted with the words of God. ³ But what if they were unfaithful to this trust? Could their unfaith frustrate the faith of God? ⁴ No! Let it be said that God remained true, even when men lied, just as it is written: That you may be justified when you speak and prevail when you are judged.

⁵ Now if our being in the wrong merely proves that God is in the right, then what shall we say? Is God unjust for punishing us? I'm reducing this to a human argument. ⁶ The answer of course is "no!" For how then would God judge the world? ⁷ But if his truth abounds even more through my lie, then why am I still judged for my sin? ⁸ And why not do wrong so that good may come? Some have blasphemed and accused us of teaching this very thing, but their condemnation is just!

17. Now to the one who calls himself a Jew.

It is uncertain at what point in history Israelites as a whole were first called by the term "Jew," meaning "praised."¹⁴ According to Josephus they derived their name from Judas Maccabeus, while Calvin and others held that in the dispersion the exiles collectively assumed the name of Judah, their most privileged tribe.

18. You have known his will...

The Jew, above all others, was uniquely positioned to know God's will, and to act as a light for other nations. Jesus himself had taught that salvation would come "through the Jews,"¹⁵ which is precisely the claim being made by Paul's opponent.

It is important to note that Paul nowhere contests the Jewish claim that they had been called by God to act as a light to the world, for he too was a Jew. The problem, as Paul points out, is that despite having the law, the

---

¹⁴ Cf. Genesis 29:35, where after the birth of her fourth son, Leah names him yehūdah ("praised"), saying "This time I will praise Yahweh."
¹⁵ Cf. John 4:22, *"salvation is (out) of the Jews"*

Jew had been ensnared by the same enemy as those to whom they were sent, and that enemy is sin.

The issue was not with the Torah or Judaism, but with Israel itself, who wrestled with the same problem as other nations, seeing as they too were *in Adam*. Just as the High Priest offered sacrifices for his own sins before he could offer them for the people,[16] Israel was now in need of the same redemption that it was charged with bringing to others.

23. Though you boast in the law, you have dishonored God by breaking it!

Paul here inveighs against Israel's failure to confront the tension between its vocation as a light to the world and its reality as a nation in sin. Because they now possessed a law that they could not keep, and a standard they could not uphold, they were no better off than those who had neither to speak of.

24. His very name is blasphemed among the nations because of you.

Paul is here citing Isaiah 52:5, where God is being mocked by other nations because of Israel's exile. This is only relevant if one remembers that the Jews of Paul's day were still living under Roman rule. For that reason, many did not feel that their exile had truly ended, even though they had physically returned home.[17]

25. Now circumcision is profitable if you keep the rest of the law...

Though circumcision was the visible sign of God's covenant with Abraham, its significance as a rite for non-Jewish followers of Jesus was highly debated in the early church.

Israel had likewise been warned that in spite of their physical circumcision, God would see them as an uncircumcised people if they continued in their sin (c.f. Jeremiah 9:25–26). This is the clear message that Paul is giving his

---

[16] Cf. Hebrews 7:27
[17] Cf. Nehemiah 9.36; Ezra 9.8–9; Tobit 14.5–7; Baruch 3.6–8

Jewish readers as well—"If you break the law then your circumcision has become uncircumcision."

26. If those who are uncircumcised fulfill the law...

The implications of Paul's teachings are that (1) the law is now being fulfilled in a new way (cf. Rom. 8:3–4, 13:8), (2) circumcision itself is being redefined (cf. Col. 2:11; Rom. 2:29), and (3) righteousness, as a status of inclusion, is being conferred by God apart from works or culture.

29. And their circumcision a matter of the heart and the spirit...

Circumcision of the heart is not a New Testament concept but appears as early as Deuteronomy 30:6, and later in Jeremiah 4:3–4. It is spoken of by Ezekiel also as God removing the heart of stone from his people and replacing it with a heart of flesh (cf. Ez. 36:26–27).

1. Then what more does the Jew have than others?

What advantage was there in being a Jew if the Jew was in the same predicament as everyone else? Paul argues that the honor of the Jew was in being called by God to act as his covenant-keeping people in the world, and the ones through whom he would bring his saving light to others.

3. But what if they were unfaithful to this trust? Could their unfaith frustrate the faith of God?

Paul here draws a sharp line between the faithfulness of God and the infidelity or unfaithfulness of human beings. Israel's failure was not simply a failure to believe but a failure to uphold God's covenant. And this failure had the outer appearance of frustrating God's plan to use them as his chosen agents in the world.

The name that Paul gives to their particular failure is "apistia," which means "unfaith," or refusing to honor a trust (cf. Rom. 3:3). A faithful Israel would have drawn the other nations to itself and to the worship of its God. Instead, other nations now looked upon the disobedience of the exiled Israelite and blasphemed the God they claimed to worship.

This paradoxical relation between the unfaith of Israel and the faithfulness of God creates the very problem that Paul wrestles with throughout much of Romans.

4. Let it be said that God remained true, even when men lied...

As Paul elsewhere writes: "Even if we are faithless, he remains faithful still, for he cannot deny himself" (2 Tim. 2:13).

> Despite man's failings, I will not withdraw my grace, nor allow my faithfulness to fail. I will not break my covenant, nor alter the word that has gone forth from my lips. (Psa. 89:33–34)

That you may be justified when you speak and prevail when you are judged.

Paul is here drawing from Psalm 51:4, where David declares that God is free of all blame when he judges sin.

5. Is God unjust for punishing us?

Calvin believed there was a possible allusion here to Genesis 18:25, where Abraham, in response to God's intent to judge Sodom, says: "Far be it from you! Will not the Judge of all the earth do right?"

8. Why not do wrong so that good may come?

The danger in presenting a doctrine of complete grace to people who have no real desire to change is that such people will often continue in sin while claiming to be under grace.

Some have blasphemed and accused us of teaching this very thing, but their condemnation is just!

Paul's wording in Greek can infer either the condemnation of the speakers (as in ESV and KJV), or the condemnation of their words (as in Phillips). Either way Paul is clear that the argument that grace has created a license to sin is without any basis in fact. "For I am not without law towards God," he writes elsewhere, "but under law towards Christ." (1 Cor. 9:21).

IV

THE RIGHTEOUSNESS OF GOD

Romans 3:9–31

[9] What then? Are we better off than others? No! Both Jews and Greeks are equally under sin. [10] Even as it is written:

> There is none righteous, not one: [11] none who understand, nor seek God. [12] All have deviated and become useless. There is no one left who does well, not even one. [13] Their throat is an opened grave; their tongues are deceiving; the poison of venomous snakes is under their lips. [14] Their mouths are full of cursing and bitterness. [15] Their feet swift to shed blood. [16] ruin and devastation are in their wake, [17] for they have not known the way of peace. [18] Nor is there any fear of God in them.

[19] Now what the law says, it is saying to those who are under the law itself, so that every mouth may be stopped, and all the world made answerable to God. [20] For no flesh shall be justified in his presence, even by acts of the law, seeing as it is through the law that we are convinced of sin.

[21] But now the righteousness that comes from God is made known to us apart from the law—though even the law and the prophets bear witness to it. [22] This righteousness has been established through the faithfulness of Jesus Christ, for the good of all those who have faith. For there is no difference between us, [23] seeing as all have sinned and fallen short of God's glory. [24] By his grace alone are we declared just through the redemption that is in Christ Jesus, [25] who God has

set forth as the seat of mercy, through his faithfulness and by his own blood. His sacrifice shows that God was not unjust in passing over the sins of the past, ²⁶ for they too were reckoned in Christ's sacrifice. And through his righteousness, God shows himself just, and the justifier of those who trust in the faithfulness of Jesus.

²⁷ On what grounds can we now boast of being in the right? None! Through what law? That of works? No! But through the law of faith. ²⁸ For we have already concluded that men are declared righteous by faith alone, and without works of the law. ²⁹ Or is he the God of the Jews only? Is he not also the God of the Nations? Yes, he is the God of the Nations also, ³⁰ for God is one, and justifies both the circumcised and uncircumcised by faith. ³¹ Are we now putting aside the law by our faith? No! But by our faith we are establishing it!

◆ ◆ ◆ ◆ ◆ ◆

10–12. Even as it is written: There is none righteous, not one.

Paul is here citing from Psalm 14:1–3 (repeated in Psalm 53:1–3), cf. "There is not a righteous man on earth who does good all of the time and does not sin" (Ecclesiastes 7:20).

Nor seek God.

That none seek God likely means that there are none who seek him for his own sake or without first being drawn by God himself, cf. "For no one can come to me, unless the Father draws them" (Jn. 6:44).

13. Their throat is an opened grave; their tongues are deceiving…

Quoted from Psalm 5:9.

14. Their mouths full of cursing and bitterness.

Quoted from Psalm 10:7.

15–17. Their feet swift to shed blood…

Quoted from Isaiah 59:7–8.

18. Nor is there any fear of God in them.

Quoted from Psalm 36:1.Together these passages are some of the most forceful in Scripture regarding the depravity of man. Sin, as Scripture bears witness, has affected all parts of the human being, i.e., his intellect, emotions, volition (will), and personality. Depravity is total in the sense that it (1) affects all aspects of man, as well as (2) all people.

21–22. But now...

The words "now" and "but now" appear throughout Romans signifying logical transitions in Paul's arguments, as well as historical shifts between what *was* and what *is*.

God's wrath was unveiled, man was condemned, sin reigned, the law governed, and we were apart. But now (!!!), God's righteousness is unveiled (3:21), we are set free (6:22), we are in Christ (8:1), and we serve God in the new way of the Spirit (7:6).

The words "but now" signify God's answer to not only human failure and sin but to legalism, self-righteousness, and human works as well.

The righteousness that comes from God.

Paul now returns to the central theme of his letter—*the righteousness of God*, laying out the following points:

(1) The gospel is God's power to save all those who have faith. (2) people are saved because they are declared to be just by God. (3) This status of being just (righteous) is conferred on those who trust in Jesus.[18] (4) The just (meaning the "righteous ones") are those who now live by faith.

The word "righteousness" appears throughout Romans[19] as a referent for both the personal righteousness of God and the status conferred on the people of faith. In some verses the term possibly indicates both ideas. What

---

[18] Cf. Philippians 3:9, where Paul contrasts *"my own righteousness"* with *"the righteousness of God by faith."*
[19] Cf. Romans 1:17; 3:5, 21, 22, 25, 26; 10:3

is clear is that God freely confers righteousness on sinners by grace, accepts it alone in salvation, and declares it alone as the basis of justification.

Made known to us apart from the law.

Paul wants his readers to know that the righteousness of God cannot be earned by ceremonial observance, ethnic descent, culture, or acts of religion. Leaving no room for personal boasting or works, what God offers us in their place is a righteousness based on grace alone.

Through the faithfulness of Jesus Christ.

In Paul's original Greek, the faith (or *faithfulness*) of Jesus can either refer to the faithfulness of Jesus himself, or the faith of those who place their trust in Jesus as Lord. The idea in most places seems to be that of a personal faith held in Jesus, though a strong case can be made in some places for the other reading as well.

For there is no difference between us...

All divisions by which we have divided our modern world, e.g., differences of race, nationality, class, culture, etc., are subsumed in the basic division of Jew and Gentile, the two categories into which first century Jews divided all human beings.

23. Seeing as all have sinned and fallen short of God's glory.

While ancient writers used the word sin to denote the action of an archer missing their intended mark, Aristotle and others used it to refer to the inherent error or flaw in the human soul. The exact meaning that Paul intends varies on the context, though here it clearly denotes the action of human beings "missing the mark" of God's glory.

The verb tenses that Paul uses in this verse suggest a correlation between acts of sin in the past and the continuing effects of sin in the present. All have sinned (past tense), he writes, and are falling short (present tense) as a result.

24. By his grace alone are we declared just...

Grace here denotes the unrecompensed favor of God towards man. That we are declared righteous means that we are now acquitted of all wrongs, justified, and regarded as innocent before God.

As Calvin and many of the early reformers taught, it is a person's status, not their character, that immediately changes when they are justified, though the transformation of one's personality, character, and will should also follow over time.

25. Who God has set forth as the seat of mercy.

Paul now draws upon the language and imagery of the altar. By hilastērion, which I've translated "seat of mercy," he means that God has made Jesus the *place* where atoning sacrifice happens. The KJV translates this as "propitiation," meaning that by which God's wrath is appeased, and the RSV as "expiation," meaning that which removes sin or guilt.

In the Septuagint, the hilastērion ("mercy seat") rested on top of the ark of the covenant, which held the broken tablets of the law given to Moses on Sinai (Exodus 25:17). Once a year the high priest entered the most sacred place in the temple with sacrificial blood and sprinkled it upon the mercy seat as an atonement for the sins of the nation. When God looked down upon the ark, he no longer acknowledged the broken tablets of the law, but the atoning blood sprinkled on the mercy seat instead.

> For the life of the flesh is in the blood, and I have given it
> to you upon the altar to make atonement for your souls.
> (Lev. 17:11)

The Bible is clear that the sacrificial blood of bulls and goats offered in the Old Testament never truly removed sin from the people who offered them (Hebrews 10:4). The removal of sin happens at the Cross alone, and in Christ alone. All previous sacrifices were a shadow of this sacrifice, and this one lamb, who alone takes away sin (cf. Jn. 1:29).

26 God shows himself just, and the justifier of those who trust in the faithfulness of Jesus.

Paul here describes God as *dikaion* (just), as well as *dikaiounta* (justifying), which is Paul's way of describing how God justifies even the worst of sinners without becoming unjust for doing so. The unique characteristics of Paul's teaching on justification are as follows:

> **(1)** Justification happens outside of the Law and independent of our own works (v. 21). **(2)** Justification is received through faith alone (v. 22). **(3)** Justification is for all nations (vv. 22b–23). **(4)** Justification is rendered by grace (v. 24). **(5)** Justification is redemptive in nature (vv. 24b–25). **(6)** Justification is a completely just act on the part of God (v. 26).

As our faithful high priest[20] Jesus mediates between God and man,[21] taking our judgment upon himself and offering his own blood in place of ours (Hebrews 10:10–12). In doing so, he offers redemptive grace and forgiveness to those who accept his actions on their behalf, and vindicates the Person and Justice of God himself for acquitting the guilty.

27. On what grounds can we now boast....

One of the greatest distinctives of Paul's writing is the thoroughness with which he dismantles the idol of human achievement. While most relish the idea of being freely forgiven, we are not without our pride, and have largely insisted on some form of rule-keeping as a part of salvation. This of course negates the real meaning of grace altogether.

28. By faith alone, and without works of the law.

Paul is not minimizing the importance of morality or good works, or suggesting that works are unnecessary, for we are created in Christ for the very purpose of them (cf. Eph. 2:10). His point rather, is that good works,

---

[20] Heb. 2:17; 4:14–16

[21] 1 Tim. 2:5

even when performed reasonably well, will not make us right with God, i.e., they will not save us.

From the vantage of the believer, works are an answer given to grace but not its cause. Grace alone is the basis given by God for salvation, and faith alone the means for appropriating grace.

30. God is one, and justifies both the circumcised and uncircumcised by faith.

Paul's point is that if there is only one God then there can only be one kind of righteousness and one manner of faith. The way he justifies one nation or group is in principle the same way he justifies another.

31. Are we now putting aside the law by our faith? No! But by our faith we are establishing it!

Paul concludes this section by affirming that we are establishing the law through the medium of faith. As his primary proof he is going to use the example of Abraham, who by faith establishes the single pattern of righteousness with God, and by whom God establishes the single pattern of faithfulness with man.

V

JUSTIFICATION AND FAITH

Romans 4:1–25

4 What shall we say about our father Abraham? What was it that he found? [2] If his righteousness was a matter of works, then he would have had reason to boast. [3] But what does the scripture say? Abraham had faith in God, and it was counted to him as righteousness. [4] Now if one works, the reward is not a matter of grace, but earned. [5] But if there is no work, but faith in the one who justifies the ungodly, then it is faith alone that is counted as righteousness. [6] In this same way David speaks of the blessing of those declared just without works, [7] saying:

> Blessed are they whose transgressions are forgiven; whose sins are covered. [8] Blessed is the man to whom the LORD does not impute sin.

[9] Is this blessing for the circumcision only, or the uncircumcised as well? We have already shown that Abraham was counted righteous by faith. [10] Was he circumcised or uncircumcised when it happened? I assure you that he was uncircumcised. [11] Circumcision, which he received afterward, was a sign of the covenant status he had already received by faith. This happened while he was uncircumcised, that he might be the father of all those who believe, whether circumcised or not. And that righteousness might come to all people, [12] not just the circumcised, but those who walk in the faith held by Abraham before his circumcision.

[13] The promise that he should afterward be heir of the world was not given to him through the law, but through the covenant status he received by faith. [14] So if we are now heirs through the law, then faith has become meaningless, and the

promise empty. [15] For the threat of the law is punishment; but where the law is absent so is the transgression.

[16] The promise then is based on faith, that all the seed might receive it by grace—not simply those having the law, but those having the faith of Abraham, who is the father of us all.[17] For to him God said: I have made you a father of many nations. And he held his faith in the presence of God, who gives life to the dead, and calls into existence things that do not exist.

[18] Against all reason to hope, Abraham hoped; believing he would be a father of many nations according to the word of God: so shall your seed be. [19] Though he was nearly a hundred years old when God spoke—his own body near death and Sarah's womb barren, he did not waver in uncertainty, but had faith. [20] He did not stumble at God's promise in unbelief, but was strengthened through his faith, giving glory to God; [21] assured that he could do the very thing he promised. [22] For this reason, his faith was counted to him as righteousness.

[23] That righteousness was counted to him by faith is not recorded for his sake, [24] but for us to whom it shall also be counted through our faith in the One who raised Jesus our Lord from death; [25] who was delivered for our trespasses and raised for our justification.

1. What shall we say about our father Abraham?

If anyone in history ever had a reason to boast it would have been Abraham. But on what basis would he have boasted? Did Abraham possess virtues or qualities that made him superior to other men? Was he better than others? Paul's answer is an emphatic "no!" It was because of Abraham's faith in God that God declared him just. The calling, promise, and covenant were each a matter of God's grace in his life, and not his personal merit.

What was it that he found?

In the traditional reading, the answer given is that Abraham found himself justified by faith, which is certainly Paul's central point.

3. Abraham had faith in God, and it was counted to him as righteousness.

When Paul says that faith was counted to Abraham as righteousness, he is saying, as does Genesis 15:6, that his righteousness was credited to him and not earned. This act of "crediting" is what it means for God to call the ungodly "righteous," the dead "living," and the non-existing "existent" (cf. Rom. 4:5, 17). It means that what is declared to be true is the work of God, and not man, whether it is righteousness, life, or existence held in view.

4. Now if one works, the reward is not a matter of grace, but is earned.

What Paul is alluding to in verses 4–5 are the same themes alluded to in Genesis 15, namely grace, faith unto righteousness, and reward, which for Abraham is the single, multi-ethnic family promised to him by God.

5. Faith in the one who justifies the ungodly...

The word "ungodly" (asebēs) literally means to be without worship or reverence. It is because of their refusal to worship that God gave men over to the non-sacred forces they desired (cf. Rom. 1:28).

Abraham, by having faith in the one who sets the asebēs in the right, models the single pattern of faith for all those who now trust in Jesus.

It is faith alone that is counted as righteousness.

The paradox of a just God declaring the unjust innocent was not lost on Paul's opponents, seeing as judges who acquitted the guilty were condemned in the Torah.

> One who justifies the wicked and one who condemns the righteous, both are an abomination to the LORD. (Prov. 17:15)

> I will not justify the wicked. (Ex. 23:7, KJV)

Paul uses the exact words used to convey what God forbids in the Torah to explain what God himself has now done in the gospel, resolving the apparent paradox with a single verse–"at the appointed time, when we were without strength, Christ died for the ungodly." (Rom. 5:6).

6. David speaks of the blessing of those declared just without works...

Because of the dynamic way that God removes David's personal guilt and restores him when he sins, he now enters the chapter as a witness to God's forgiveness and justification.

7–8. Blessed are they whose transgressions are forgiven...to whom the LORD does not impute sin.

Luther taught that believers were intrinsically sinners, even while extrinsically justified. By intrinsic he meant as we are in our own strength and estimation, and by extrinsic he meant how we are in God's sight and reckoning, cf. "sinners in fact but righteous in hope."

9. Is this blessing for the circumcision only, or the uncircumcised as well?

If Abraham is our father in a physical or ethnic sense alone, then the blessing is only for those who share ethnic kinship and circumcision with him in that way, and not all families of the earth, which is God's actual promise (Gen. 12:3).

11. Circumcision, which he received afterward, was a sign of the covenant status he had already received by faith.

Though circumcision was the distinguishing mark of the Jew, Abraham was still an uncircumcised inhabitant of Ur when he first came to faith, and therefore still a virtual Gentile when God declared him righteous (Gen. 15:6).

His physical circumcision which came 14 years later was an outward sign confirming, but not conferring covenant status, and adding nothing to the righteousness already given.

13. That he should afterward be heir of the world.

The actual land promised to Abraham in Genesis was the land between Egypt and the Euphrates (Gen.15:18), and not the entire world, as Paul suggests in this verse. In the spiritual sense in which he interprets the promise however, the physical land now becomes the entire redeemed cosmos, new creation, cf. "the heavenly city."[22]

14. If we are now heirs through the law, then faith has become meaningless...

To subject the fulfillment of God's promises to the ups and downs of our own obedience would make the fulfillment of those promises tenuous at best. And if we are made heirs through the law alone, then God's word is dependent on us – *and not God* – for its fulfillment.

15. For the threat of the law is punishment; but where the law is absent so is the transgression.

Paul is not claiming that there is no sin in the absence of law, but distinguishing sin itself, which is everywhere present, from transgression, which only exists where a law or commandment is known and willfully broken. Therefore, there is no transgression in the absence of a revealed law, although sin itself will remain.

This is Paul's point in 5:13 as well: "sin was already present in the world before the law, but sin, where there was no law, was not reckoned."

16. The promise then is based on faith, that all the seed might receive it by grace...

In Galatians, Paul uses the term seed as a referent for both Christ (Gal. 3:16) and his people, who are now heirs according to the promise (Gal. 3:29). His point here is that what is promised must be received through faith.

17. Who gives life to the dead...

There is an allusion here to Abraham, who considered his body nearly dead, and Sarah, whose womb was barren.[23] In giving Abraham and Sarah

---

[22] "they desire a better *country*, that is, a heavenly one." (Heb. 11:16, NASB)

[23] Cf. 4:19, "...his own body near death and Sarah's womb barren (Grk. *nekrōsis*, "*in deadness*").

the ability to birth nations from their own bodies, God was essentially giving life to what had been dead.

18. Abraham hoped; believing he would be a father of many nations according to the word of God...

In the context of the Old Testament, the nations over which Abraham is called a father are comprised of his offspring through Isaac (Israel and Edom), Ishmael (Gen. 25:12–18), and Keturah (Gen. 25:2–4). In the New Testament, however, his offspring is comprised of all those who have come to faith in Christ.

So shall your seed be.

Quoted from Genesis 15:5, where God likens Abraham's future seed, or family, to the stars in heaven. This promise is traditionally understood numerically, with the stars reflecting the number of Abraham's future descendants. Some early interpreters understood the promise to be qualitative also, meaning not just about the numeric expansion of Abraham's future seed, but about its transformation as well.

20. He did not stumble at God's promise in unbelief, but was strengthened through his faith...

There are only two real responses to divine promise: one can either judge or critique the promise or glorify the one who promised. While the former may result in doubt or unbelief, the latter brings about hope and rejoicing in the present.

25. Who was delivered for our trespasses and raised for our justification.

Allowing room for Paul's other arguments, this is really the central point of the letter itself, i.e., Christ was delivered for our trespasses and raised for our justification.

VI

TRIUMPHANT GRACE

Romans 5:1–21

5 Having been justified by faith we now have peace with God through our Lord Jesus Christ. ² And by faith we access the grace to stand and rejoice in the hope of God's glory.

³ And not only in this hope, but we rejoice in our suffering also, knowing that our suffering produces patience, ⁴ our patience produces character; and our character—when it has been formed by the things we endure, produces more hope. ⁵ And hope does not lead us to frustration, seeing as God's love is poured out in us through the Holy Spirit.

⁶ And this is the work of Christ: That at the appointed time, when we were without strength, he died for the ungodly. ⁷ And though most would be unwilling to die, even for a good person, ⁸ God has shown his great love for us through Christ, who died for us while we were still in sin.

⁹ Having now justified us by his blood, how much more will he also deliver us from wrath? ¹⁰ And though we were at enmity with God, he has reconciled us to himself through the dying of his son. How much more, being reconciled through his dying, shall we be saved through his life? ¹¹ Therefore we rejoice in God through our Lord Jesus Christ, through whom we are reconciled unto God.

¹² Now sin entered our world through one man, and his sin brought death, and this death spread to all men—*because all sinned.* ¹³ And though sin entered before the law, it remained unreckoned in the absence of law itself. ¹⁴ Still, death reigned from Adam to Moses, even over those who did not sin in the same manner as Adam, who is the type of the one to come.

[15] The latter's gift however, is unlike the former's trespass. For if many died through Adam, the gift of God through Christ abounded even more to the many. [16] And what is given in grace is unlike what is received through the trespass. For the judgment which followed one trespass resulted in condemnation, but the gift which follows many trespasses has resulted in justification. [17] So if death reigned through the trespass of one, how much more shall grace and the gift of righteousness reign through the life of the other?

[18] Just as one trespass brought us all into condemnation, so one act of righteousness has brought us into justification and life. [19] And as many were made sinners through the disobedience of one, many are now made righteous through the obedience of the other.

[20] The law entered that the trespass might reach its full extent. But where sin abounded, grace abounded even more. [21] And where sin reigned in death, grace now reigns in life through the righteousness of our Lord, Jesus Christ.

———————— ✦✦✦✦✦ ————————

1. Having been justified by faith we now have peace with God through our Lord Jesus...

The Greek word for "peace" (eirēnē) is derived from a verb that means to join or bring together and denotes the "coming together" of essential parts, in this case God and man.

The peace we now have *in Christ* is a direct result of the peace we have *through Christ*, and includes all that is implied by the Hebrew word "shalom" (peace), i.e., wholeness, prosperity, health, wellbeing, etc.

2. And by faith we access the grace to stand and rejoice in the hope of God's glory.

One of the most powerful images of the believer's access in Christ is found at the crucifixion when Jesus releases his spirit at death. When he releases his spirit the veil that hangs in the Temple is torn from top to bottom.[24] The meaning of the split veil is connected to the function of the veil itself, which was to separate humanity from God's presence in the Temple.

---

[24] Cf. Matthew 27:51; Mark 15:38; Luke 23:45

And rejoice in the hope of God's glory.

To "rejoice" meant to celebrate or lift one's head in triumph or boast, and describes the confidence we now have in Jesus.

Although it is called hope, our future expectation is certain, seeing as we have already received the guarantee of its realization through the indwelling of the Spirit, who Paul also refers to as the "earnest" or "guarantee of our inheritance" (Eph. 1:14, BLB).

3. We rejoice in our suffering also...

Paul does not say that we rejoice *because* of our suffering, but that we rejoice *in it*. Suffering was often the normal experience of believers, and in some ways, part of the Christian vocation itself. Paul considered it to be a vital part of following Jesus in this world, cf. Colossians 1:24.

3-4. The reason we can rejoice in our suffering, is because we know that God is using it to bring about our own patience, character, and hope (cf. Job 23:10; James 1:2-4; Heb. 12), as well as the furtherance of his divine purpose in our lives and in the world.

5. And hope does not lead to frustration, seeing as God's love is poured out in us through the Holy Spirit

This is the first formal mention Paul makes of the Holy Spirit, who is introduced as the one pouring out the love of God within us.

6. The appointed time

The "appointed time" refers to time as it is allotted in God's will and purpose, and not ours, cf. "the present time" (3:26), "the fulness of time" (Gal. 4:4), "these last times" (1 Pet. 1:20).

9. Having now justified us by his blood...

While "blood" may be a referent to the atoning death of Jesus, it is also a characteristic way of speaking about his life, which was poured out for sin (cf. Isa. 53:12). In the Old Covenant, the life of the flesh (and not its death) was represented by the blood (cf. Lev. 17:11).

How much more will he also deliver us from wrath?

Paul here infers the future blessing of those justified by faith in the present. Jesus not only delivers us in the present, but from that which is still future, i.e., "the wrath to come" (1 Thess. 1:10).

10. He has reconciled us to himself.

The Bible is clear that it is man who has been reconciled to God, and not God who has been reconciled to man. The hostility that needed to be removed was within men, not within God. For it is we who had turned away from him, and not he who turned away from us.

How much more, being reconciled through his dying, shall we be saved through his life?

By "life" Paul means the risen life of Christ, which is made our life as well through the indwelling of his Spirit.[25] he alone is our resurrection and life (Jn. 11:25), and through him alone do we receive sanctifying grace and deliverance in the present, as well as glorification in the future.

12. Now sin entered our world through one man, and his sin brought death.

Paul now brings all that has been said to a point by contrasting two very different types of humanity, i.e., the first Adam and the last Adam, which is Christ, cf. "For as all die in Adam, so in Christ all are made alive" (1 Cor. 15:22).

If we are going to understand the role of "Adam" in redemptive history, then we will have to first consider the meaning of the word *adam* itself.

When the name Adam appears in the Hebrew text of Genesis it usually has the definite article in front of it, and reads *ha adam*, meaning "the man"

---

[25] Cf. Gal. 5:25 *"Since we live by the Spirit, let us walk in step with the Spirit."*

or "the human." In Jewish thought, Adam was both an individual person and at times a corporate personality, with humanity as a whole being represented in him. Paul adds to this by referring to Adam as a pattern or type of the one to come, which is Jesus the Messiah.

Though Eve's sin was first in order (she ate of the fruit in the garden prior to Adam), Adam is held liable for several reasons. Firstly, as the head of the species, and the one to whom God had spoken, he was responsible for both himself and the human family (cf. Gen. 2:18–23; 1 Cor. 11:3). Secondly, it was Eve who was deceived by the serpent (1 Tim. 2:14), and not Adam. His sin is a willing transgression against God's word, and not the result of a deception.

> O Adam, what have you done? For though it was you who sinned, the fall was not yours alone, but ours also who are your descendants.[26]

This death spread to all men—*because all sinned.*

The "death" first spoken of in Genesis 2:17[27] was more than the dissolution of life held in the physical body. For Paul, death was a kind of regenerate force, opposing life itself, and defacing the original goodness found in God's creation.

13–14. Paul here has in mind the question of those who lived between Adam and Moses, i.e., those who lived before the law was given on Sinai. Because death (which is far more than simply *dying*) was already present, Paul argues that sin too must have already been present as well.

In Judaism many teachers held that the seven commandments given to Noah after the flood were binding on all subsequent human beings, seeing as the latter division between Jew and Gentile did not yet exist when they were given (cf. Genesis 9:1–7). Though Paul never mentions these commandments specifically, most of them were present in the

---

[26] 2 Esdras 7:118, NRSA
[27] "*for in the day that you eat of it you shall surely die*" (Gen. 2:17, ESV)

commands first given to Adam, *e.g.*, Be fruitful, multiply, replenish, etc. (cf. Gen. 1:26–28).

Adam, who is the type of the one to come.

For Paul, Adam here represents humanity itself, as does Jesus, through whom the image of the *fallen adam* is replaced with the reality of the *risen adam*, cf. "The first Adam became a living being, but the last Adam, a life-giving spirit" (1 Cor. 15:45).

15. The latter's gift however, is unlike the former's trespass.

The words "unlike," "even more," and "the other" (vv. 15–17) highlight the dissimilarity between the trespass of men and the grace of God, i.e., that which ushers in condemnation and that which brings life.

His point is that there is a dissimilarity between the gift and the transgression. The effect of one (grace) is exceedingly greater ("even more") than the other (sin). Put differently, there is more abundant grace found in Jesus than condemnation found in Adam. In dying, Christ not only cancels the effects of the latter's sin but provides us with something even greater than what was lost.

16. What is given in grace is unlike what is received through the trespass.

"The many offenses from which we are freed through Christ are not limited to those committed before our baptism, but also those by which the saints daily contract new guilt; and on account of which they would be justly condemned, were they not continually relieved by this grace."[28]

17. How much more shall grace and the gift of righteousness reign through the life of the other?

Paul uses the verb basileúō ("to rule as a king") here and in 5:21 to describe God's kingdom in Christ prevailing over the world's powers.

---

[28] John Calvin

18. One trespass brought us all into condemnation…

In many ways, Paul is retelling the story of Israel through the story of Adam and bringing both narratives to their intended end in Jesus. The parallels between Adam's fall and Israel's exile are obvious to the careful student.

- God's command for Adam to be fruitful and multiply translates into his promise to multiply and bless Israel.
- The garden in Eden becomes the land of promise in the story of Israel. Like the garden, the land of promise is the place of blessing, fellowship, and intimacy with God.
- Adam's expulsion from Eden prefigures Israel's exile from Canaan.

For Paul, it is the Messiah who now takes upon himself the vocation of Israel, who reverses the consequences of Adam's sin in Eden, and sums up in himself the new humanity—*or Adam.*

If we fail to recognize the Adamic pattern repeated in the life of Israel, or the dynamic fashion that Israel's Messiah takes upon himself the history, vocation, and calling of the entire nation, then we risk misunderstanding the biblical narrative altogether, and much of what Paul has to say about Adam, Israel, and Christ.

19. Many are now made righteous through the obedience of the other.

Paul may be echoing Isaiah 53:11, where God declares that his servant "will justify many" and "bear their iniquities." Here, as in Isaiah, the servant's obedience is how others are now made just, cf. "we have now been justified by his blood" (Rom. 5:9, KJV).

20. That the trespass might reach its full extent.

One of the purposes of the Law was to illuminate the sin of Adam's seed. Though holy, righteous, and good (Rom. 7:12), the law has the peculiar effect of arousing in us the very sin it condemns, which is the point of Galatians 3:19 as well: "Why then the law? It was added because of transgressions."[29] Paul is clear that sin can never be abated by the law, only magnified and more clearly seen for what it truly is.

21. And where sin reigned in death, grace now reigns in life through the righteousness of our Lord, Jesus Christ.

Sin and Grace are both personified by Paul as female rulers exercising dominion over their loyal subjects. One (Sin) reigns unto death, while the other (Grace) reigns unto life through the righteousness of Jesus.

---

[29] The words *transgression* and *trespass* both imply a willful deviation from a given standard or pattern, in this case, the law or commandment of God.

VII

NEWNESS OF LIFE

Romans 6:1–23

6 What now? Shall we continue in sin so that we can receive more grace? [2] No! For how can we live any longer in sin when we have already died to it? [3] Or have you forgotten that when we were baptized into Christ Jesus we were baptized into his death? [4] That means we were buried with him in our baptism, that just as Christ was raised from the dead by the Father's glory, we too should now live in newness of life. [5] Having already been joined to him in the likeness of his death, how much more should we share in the likeness of his rising?

[6] For we know that our old humanity was crucified with Christ, that the body of sin might be rendered powerless, and we ourselves freed of its rule— [7] for in dying we have been freed.

[8] And if we died with Christ, then we have faith that we shall live with him also. [9] And since he has already been raised, we know that he is no longer subject to death—for death has no more authority over him. [10] And in dying, he died to sin once, that in living, he might live to God eternally. [11] You too, in like manner, are to now reckon yourselves dead to sin, that you might live unto God in Christ Jesus.

[12] No longer allow sin to reign in your mortal bodies, nor submit yourselves to its desires, [13] nor surrender your limbs to unrighteousness. But give yourselves to God as those who have been raised from death and present your limbs to him in righteousness. [14] For sin has no more authority over those who are no longer under the law, but under grace.

[15] What then? Should we sin even more because we are under grace and not the law? No! [16] Don't you realize that you are the slave of whatever it is you obey—whether

sin, which ends in death, or the obedience *of faith*, which ends in righteousness? [17] Thank God that although you were once servants of sin, your hearts have now yielded to the pattern of teaching given to you; [18] being loosed from the power of sin, and made servants of righteousness. [19] I am using human terms because of the weakness of your flesh. Just as you were once servants of uncleanness and given to what is unlawful; yield yourselves to what is righteous and submit to what is holy.

[20] For when you were enslaved by sin, you were without righteousness. [21] What fruit did you bear then, other than what brought shame and death? [22] But now, being freed from sin and made servants of God, you have born the fruit of holiness unto everlasting life! [23] For the wages earned by sin are death; but the gift which is given to us by God is eternal life through Christ Jesus, our Lord.

<hr />

1. Shall we continue in sin so that we can receive more grace?

Paul's question is rhetorical, and aimed at those who had willingly misrepresented the gospel and its emphasis on grace, using both as an occasion to continue in sin.

2. No! For how can we live any longer in sin when we have already died to it?

Paul does not say that believers will never sin, nor does he suggest that sin will no longer appeal to followers of Jesus at a base level. Rather, he states that it is unnecessary for those risen in Jesus to live their lives in submission to sin any longer.

3. We were baptized into his death.

What is historically true of Jesus becomes true of us as well when we accept his death and resurrection as our own, cf. "I am crucified with Christ, and yet I still live" (Gal. 2:20).

Our personal identification with Christ in death and resurrection is symbolized more in physical baptism than perhaps any other rite, though Paul's point is more about our actual union than the details of baptism.

Though it is evident from Acts that it was the normative practice of the church to baptize members immediately upon their confession of faith, it is equally clear that it was their faith in Jesus, and not their physical baptism in water, that brought salvation, and the indwelling Spirit.[30]

4. Christ was raised from the dead by the Father's glory.

In the context of Christ's resurrection, the Father's glory, which Paul elsewhere calls "the working of his might," is the Power that he displays in raising Jesus from the dead (cf. Eph. 1:19–20).

We too should now live in newness of life.

Through the giving of the Holy Spirit God has implanted the life of his Son Jesus in each of us, which we now access through our faith in the same power that raised him from the dead (cf. Col. 2:12).

It is not a metaphor or allegory that Paul is introducing here, but a simple fact–Jesus Christ, the Son of God, lives in every one of us who calls on him in faith, and his life within us is not without effect.

It was one thing to believe the "right" things about God and Christ, and another to "walk" in them. Paul is adamant that as disciples of Jesus we must do both.

5. How much more should we share in the likeness of his rising?

Beza, often called the successor to Calvin in the Swiss Reformation, held that Paul used the words "should we," because we were not yet wholly dead to the flesh, nor wholly risen in the Spirit. Rather, Beza argued, we were daily emerging as it were from one to the other. And though we now bear the life of Christ in faith, we shall later bear it with him in fact.

---

[30] "Then Peter said, "Surely no one can stand in the way of them being baptized with water, seeing that they have already received the Holy Spirit" (cf. Acts 10:44–47).

6. Our old humanity was crucified with Christ.

For Paul, the crucifixion was both an event in history and an experience by faith. "Through it," he boasts, "the world has been crucified to me, and I to the world" (Gal. 6:14). In both passages the perfect tense denotes a present experience produced by the reality of a previous one. Christ was crucified (past tense), and we now take part in that crucifixion (present tense) by faith. We should also note that it is not our physical bodies, or even our appetites, that are made powerless by the cross, but the fallen nature to which our physical bodies were subjected in Adam.

7. For in dying we have been freed.

When one dies, they are no longer liable for the debts they incurred during their lifetime, for the dead can no longer pay such debts, and are therefore free of them. In this same manner, those crucified with Jesus are now free from the debt they have incurred through sin.

8. We shall live with him also.

Those who have died in Jesus now live with him by faith and through the Spirit but will afterward live with him in the fulness of all that implies.

10. He died to sin once.

Christ's victory is conclusive, leaving no second fight, and no second foe.

11. Reckon yourselves dead to sin...

To reckon themselves dead to sin, yet alive to Christ, was no mere act of the imagination or will, but an exercise in divine reasoning empowered by the Spirit, whose presence enabled a very real sense of their identity in Jesus.

For Paul, reckoning was about an alteration of our thoughts and awareness. His readers were being asked to reason certain things out, with or without an accompanying emotion or change of sentiment. Those baptized were now being invited to consider their faith, and to work out the following points in their own minds:

(1) Jesus died to sin. (2) Jesus rose to God. (3) We are united to Jesus by faith and baptism. Therefore, (4) we too have died to sin. (5) We too have also risen to God.

Unto God in Christ Jesus.

These five words in Greek (tō Theō en Christō Iēsou) are a summation of everything that Paul has taught up to this point. We are "unto" God, but only because we are "in" Christ. This is the gospel!

13. Give yourselves to God.

The believer's body—through faith and the in-dwelling Spirit, is now a temple for the living God (cf. 1 Cor. 6:19–20). Their limbs are likewise reckoned as instruments for God's use. In a proper sense, the believer's body is now a tool for building God's kingdom, a weapon for warring against the influence of the Satan, and an implement for harvesting God's fields.

14. Those who are no longer under the law, but under grace.

We should not think that Paul is here pitting God's law against his grace, for both equally belong to God. Nor should we think that there was no grace to be had under Moses. For the covenant at Sinai begins with an act of grace ("I am Yahweh who brought you out of Egypt"), and only afterward introduces obligation, blessing, and cursing, cf. Ex. 20:2; Deut. 5:6; 11:26-28; 32:47.

15. Should we sin even more because we are under grace and not the law?

To treat grace as an excuse to continue in sin was proof for Augustine that one had not really received grace to begin with. For to receive grace was to receive the life of the grace giver as well, i.e., Jesus, and to receive Jesus was to be free of sin.

16. Don't you realize that you are the slave of whatever it is you obey?

One is the servant of whatever they have obeyed, for obedience is a sign of the authority held by the one to whom it is given. This was Calvin's argument on the matter. His point is that to obey sin is to be its servant.

17. The pattern of teaching given to you.

The doctrine or pattern of teaching referred to by Paul is likely synonymous with what he elsewhere calls the traditions or teachings delivered to the various churches through oral instructions and epistles (cf. 1 Cor. 11:2; 2 Thes. 2:15).

18. Being loosed from the power of sin.

The word "loosed" or "set free" (ESV) describes the release of Paul's readers from the actual dominion of sin, and not simply its guilt, as in verse 7.

19. I am using human terms, because of the weakness of your flesh.

Cf. "your natural limitations" (ESV), "what is proportionable to man's strength" (Chrysostom), "what is moderate" (Hammond). Paul admits that his analogy is imperfect, for in writing he has accommodated himself to the understanding of his readers, and this often requires, as he sometimes notes, the use of imperfect language and metaphors.

21. What fruit did you bear then, other than what brought shame and death?

Paul's readers had reaped no real benefit from their previous sin, other than things which they were now ashamed of. The fruit of holiness, or sanctification infers the process by which Paul's readers were now advancing in a progressive demonstration of the resurrection.

23. For the wages earned by sin are death; but the gift which is given to us by God is eternal life...

The word wage indicated "payment for work done." For Paul, sin was like a kind of work that man labored at in exchange for death. A gift, which is another way of saying "extended grace," suggests a divine gratuity, or endowment, completely unearned by its recipient. It can also include deliverance from danger or passion, as well as God's influence upon the heart.

Man's rights extend only as far as death, seeing it is an earned wage, and thence rightfully his. It is only when he abandons his rights however and releases his hold on the just payment for his sin, that he can receive the gift extended to him by grace, which is life.

VIII

THE LAW AND THE SPIRIT

Romans 7:1–25

7 Dear brothers, surely those of you who are familiar with the law understand that a law only has authority over a person while they are alive? ² Just as the law can only bind a woman to her husband while he is alive. If he dies, then she is loosed from the law that bound her to him. ³ If she were to sleep with another man while he was alive she would be called an adulteress. But if he dies, then his death releases her from the law, and she is no longer called an adulteress for being with another man.

⁴ In the same way, brothers, you died to the law when you were joined with Christ in his death. And since you are now joined with him that was raised from death, you fruit is now unto God. ⁵ For when we were in the flesh the influence of sin in our limbs was aroused by the law so that we bore fruit unto death. ⁶ But now, being released from the law and having died to what held us, we serve God in the newness of the Spirit and not the old way of the letter

⁷ What then? Is the law itself sin? No! I would not have even known what sin was had it not been for the law. For if the law had not said, "do not covet," I would not have known covetousness for the wrong that it is. ⁸ But sin, stirred by the commandment, awakened in me an awareness of my own covetousness. Apart from the law, however, my awareness of sin was dead.

⁹ Before the law, I was alive; but when I received the commandment it awakened in me a consciousness of sin, and I died. ¹⁰ The commandment that pointed to life brought me to death, ¹¹ for sin itself worked through the commandment.

It deceived me and brought me to death through what was right. [12] But the law remains holy, and the commandment holy, just, and good.

[13] Did that which was good result in death? No! But sin, that it might be known, has been producing death through what is good; that through the goodness of God's commandment, sin might be made apparent.

[14] Now we know that the law is spiritual, but I'm still fleshly, and under the yoke of sin. [15] I don't even recognize my actions because they're not the things I want to do. Rather, what I'm doing are the very things I hate. [16] But if I do the things that I hate, then I agree with the law that what it says is good.

[17] It is therefore no longer I who am breaking the law, but sin dwelling in me—[18] for I know that nothing good lives in my flesh. And though I desire what is good with my thoughts, it is not the thing I do with my limbs. [19] For I don't do the things I desire to do; but instead, I do the things I hate. [20] But if I hate the things that I'm doing, then it is no longer I who am doing them, but sin living within me.

[21] So, this is what I have found regarding the law: When I desire to do what is right, evil is still with me. [22] And though I delight in the law of God, [23] there is another law working in my flesh, warring against the law in my mind; and bringing me under the dominion of sin, which is within me.

[24] How miserable of a condition I'm in! Who can deliver me from the death at work in this body? [25] I thank God, who indeed delivers us through Jesus Christ, our Lord! For with my mind, I serve the law of God, but with my flesh the law of sin.

1. Those of you who are familiar with the law...

Those familiar with either Jewish or Roman forms of law would have understood Paul's reasoning about the law's authority over a person ending at the time of their death. Just as he had previously worked out the meaning of the believer's death to sin, he now works out that of his death to the Law

2. The law can only bind a woman to her husband while he is alive. If he dies, then she is loosed from the law...

Paul's example illustrates the general principle already introduced in verse 1. His point is that death dissolves the relationships which make the law binding on us in life.

4. In the same way, brothers, you died to the law when you were joined with Christ in his death.

Since the Christian is joined to Jesus in his death, they are also loosed from the law that governed them in this life and raised with him into a new kind of existence, cf. "If you have been raised up with Christ, keep seeking the things above, where Christ is" (Col. 3:1, NASB).

5. For when we were in the flesh the influence of sin in our limbs was aroused by the law...

The NLT rightly renders the word "flesh" as "old nature," which is what Paul means when he states that we were previously "in the flesh."

6. Being released from the law and having died to what held us.

Dying to "what held us" means dying to our old nature, as well as the law to which it was subject. That we now serve in the new way of the Spirit suggests a qualitative shift in our lives, as opposed to a temporal one, i.e., something new, not merely recent.

7. Is the law itself sin?

Though the law brings an awareness of sin and even provokes it in some instances (cf. 3:20, 5:20, 7:5), the sin spoken of is still ours, and not the laws. For the law of God is holy, and its precepts holy, just, and good (7:12).

While Paul is painfully aware of the Law's ability to expose sin, he is equally aware of its inability to remove it. Its function is diagnostic, not therapeutic, meaning it exposes an illness that it cannot heal. This is the bleak picture Paul gives of life under the law—under Torah. Sin without remedy.

I would not have even known what sin was had it not been for the law.

The function of the law was to expose and make known to us the very things which we hide, even from ourselves. The exposure of sin without a true remedy is the problem of most religion as we know it.

"Do not covet."

The commandment that Paul cites is one that addresses an inner attitude, not an outward action. "Do not covet" is really a prohibition against unchecked desires and self-regarding wants that usurp the place that God alone ought to occupy in our hearts. Paul elsewhere likens this sin to idolatry (Col. 3:5).

8. But sin, stirred by the commandment, awakened in me an awareness of my own covetousness.

Paul here characterizes sin as a type of adversary or enemy – *a satan,* with which he has been wrestling. His personification of sin is consistent with Genesis 4, where sin is described as an animal-like adversary, lurking about with an inverted desire towards Cain.[31]

While the biblical writers used various words to express this reality,[32] each of them implied that man had in some way surrendered his God-given power to lesser, non-divine forces.

My awareness of sin was dead.

By dead, Paul means that his awareness of sin was absent or possibly sleep, but not completely done away with. This is clear from verse 9, where he states that his awareness of sin *revived* (KJV), *came to life* (NLT), or *awakened from death* (Constable).

---

[31] cf. *"If you do well, will you not be uplifted? But if you do not do well, then Sin lies at the opening, and its desire is to have you, but you must rule it" (Gen. 4:7).*

[32] Cf. **khatā** (sin, astray), **pesha** (transgression, trespass, deviation), **avōn** (iniquity).

9. Before the law, I was alive.

By alive, Paul means that he was without the law, i.e., ignorant of the extent and obligations of its commands, and therefore uncondemned. "I apprehended myself to be righteous, and on the way of eternal life."

10. The commandment that pointed to life brought me to death.

The commandment that pointed to life is likely Leviticus 18:5, or one similar to it, cf. "The man who does these things shall live by them."

11. [Sin] deceived me and brought me to death...

Cf. *"The serpent deceived me, and I ate"* (Gen. 3:13). Just as the serpent deceived Eve in Genesis, Paul states that he was deceived by Sin, and brought to death as a result.[33]

12. But the law remains holy, and the commandment holy, just, and good.

Paul argues that as the revelation of God's will and perfect character, the Law was holy (set apart), just (free of any wrong), good (intrinsically superior), and spiritual (belonging to a higher order).

14. But I'm still fleshly, and under the yoke of sin.

The word fleshly infers that the Adamic nature is carnal or unspiritual in relation to the Law. The idea that man lives under the authority of sin has a parallel in Wisdom 1:4, where Wisdom states that it refuses to dwell in a body "under debt" (NAB), or "mortgaged" to sin (NEB).

15. I don't even recognize my actions because they're not the things I want to do.

There are close parallels between Paul and other ancient writers in the first century who spoke of being unable to perform the moral good which they desired.

---

[33] *"In the day that you eat of it you shall die"* (Gen. 2:17).

If I could, I would act with greater wisdom, but some other force is pulling me. My desire speaks one thing, but my mind another. I see the better way and want to follow it, but I take the worse. (Ovid)

I pursue the things which have done me harm; I shun the things that will bring me good. (Horace)

20. It is no longer I who am doing them, but sin living within me.

It is important to note that Paul is not here attempting to escape responsibility for his behaviors. Rather, he is identifying the source of his trouble. It is not "I" he states, but the sin to which my Adamic nature has been subjected.

23. Another law working in my flesh, warring against the law in my mind.

The moral conflict, for Paul, was a conflict between two kinds of laws within him: (1) the law at work in his limbs, and (2) the law at work in his mind.

24. How miserable of a condition I'm in!

The word *misery* describes the condition of one afflicted or worn out from continuous struggle or conflict. For Wiersbe, it infers one who had exhausted themselves trying to please God, only to find that their best efforts had not been enough.

Calvin wrote that such misery is the plight of one panting and nearly fainting, because he has not found that for which he longs.

Who can deliver me from the death at work in this body?

It is not our justification that Paul has in view here, but our deliverance from what he calls *the body of death*, meaning the death which has infected the body.

Ancient writers like Plato, Epictetus, and Marcus Aurelius, described the human soul as being tethered to a body from which it longed to be free.

In contrast, the Christian hope was one in which the body itself was also redeemed and not simply discarded at death (cf. Rom. 8:23).

25. I thank God, who indeed delivers us through Jesus Christ.

Having cried for deliverance, the voice of Romans 7 now shouts in triumph for not just an escape from the death which has infected the body, but for an absolute and decisive victory over it in Jesus.

For with my mind, I serve the law of God, but with my flesh the law of sin.

Calvin argued that the faithful never truly arrive at their finished state of perfection while in the body or "flesh" as it now exists, hence Paul's apparent concession to the law of sin.

By "mind," Paul has in view the part of the soul that is illumined by God's Spirit, delights in God's law, and understands and wills those things that are in accord with his Word.

IX

BEING LED BY THE SPIRIT

Romans 8:1–39

8 But there is no longer any condemnation for those in Christ Jesus, [2] for whom the power of the Spirit of life has set free from the power of sin and death. [3] For God, by sending his son in a body like our own, has done for us what the law could not because of the weakness in our flesh. By condemning sin in the body of his son, [4] God himself has answered the righteous standard of the law in us who are now walking according to the Spirit, and not the flesh.

[5] For those who live by the flesh set their minds on the flesh, but those who live by the Spirit set their minds on the Spirit. [6] And though the mind given over to the flesh dies, the mind given to the Spirit lives with peace. [7] For the mind of the flesh strives against God, being unable to even discern his law, [8] and such people cannot please him.

[9] But if they have received God's Spirit in them then they are the people of the Spirit, and not the flesh. And if they have not received the Spirit–which is of Christ, then they are not his people. [10] But if he dwells in you through the Spirit, then the body dies because of sin, but the Spirit lives because of righteousness. [11] And if the same Spirit that raised Jesus now lives in you, then he that raised Christ will also restore life to your bodies through his Spirit, which is now in you as well.

[12] We are therefore in debt, but not to the life of the flesh. [13] For to live solely in the flesh is to die; but to mortify the actions of the flesh—through the life of the Spirit—is to live.

[14] And those who are now led by God's Spirit are God's children. [15] And his Spirit is not a spirit of bondage, that we should turn in fear; but the Spirit of adoption,

by whom we cry, "Abba, Father!" [16] And his Spirit now witnesses with our spirit that we are his children. [17] And if we are God's children, then we are also his heirs, being fellow heirs with Christ. For if we share in his suffering, then surely we will also share in his glory.

[18] And I reason that our present sufferings are of no comparison with the coming glory which shall be revealed in us. [19] For creation itself stirs in expectation, awaiting the unveiling of God's children. [20] It was subjected to the curse of futility, though not of its own will; but by the will of the one who subjected it in hope. [21] For creation too will be loosed from its enslavement to decay and set within the freedom revealed when God's children are finally glorified.

[22] For we know that creation is travailing, even now, as if it were in labor. [23] And not only creation, but we too, who have the first fruit of the Spirit within us, are travailing within ourselves as we await the consummation of our adoption, which is the redemption of our bodies. [24] For such is the hope of salvation. But hope, if it can be seen, would not be hope. For who would hope for what they had already seen? [25] But if we hope, then we hope for what we have not yet seen and wait for it expectantly—but with patience.

[26] In this same way, the Spirit is now joined with us—helping us in our weaknesses. For we don't always know how to pray as we should, but the Spirit intercedes for us with sighing deeper than our own words. [27] And he that searches the hearts knows every thought of the Spirit, because he intercedes for God's people according to God's will.

[28] And we know that God is bringing all things together for the good of those who love him—those who are called according to his purpose. [29] For whom he foreknew, he also predestined to be conformed to the image of his son, that he might be the firstborn among many sons and daughters. [30] And those he predestined, he also called; and those he called, he also declared just; and those he declared just, he glorified.

[31] What shall we then say? If God is for us, who can be against us? [32] For he did not withhold his own son but gave him up for us all! How then will he not also give all things to those who are now in him?

[33] Who then can accuse God's elect when it is God himself who declares them just? [34] Who is it that condemns us when it is Christ himself who died, and has been raised—and is even now seated at the right hand of God interceding for us?

[35] And what can separate us from the love of Christ? Tribulation? Anguish or persecution? Hunger, nakedness, or danger? The sword? [36] As it is written:

> For your sake we are killed all day long; and are reckoned as sheep for the slaughter.

[37] But even in these, we prevail through the power of the one who loved us. [38] And I am persuaded that neither death nor life, angels or principalities, things present or things to come; powers, [39] height, depth, or anything created, can separate us from the love of God, which is in Christ Jesus, our Lord.

———————————— ✦ ✦ ✦✦✦ ✦ ✦ ————————————

1. But there is no longer any condemnation for those in Christ Jesus.

Paul frequently uses the words "in Christ" as a spatial metaphor pointing to the new existence we now have in Jesus. For Paul, the life being shared among Christ's followers was the very life of Christ himself, and this life was to be lived out and expressed among them.

Calvin argued that Romans 8:1 was really about three points: (1) the imperfection under which the faithful now labor, (2) the mercy of God in perpetually forgiving that imperfection, and (3) the regenerating power of the Spirit within those who are yet imperfect.

2. The power of the Spirit of life…the power of sin and death.

Paul here refers to the regularity and force with which the Spirit and sin operate in our human lives. Both function according to a constancy of influence and action, which Paul calls law (Gk. nomos).

3. God, by sending his son in a body like our own, has done for us what the law could not because of the weakness in our flesh.

Although the law could not produce the life that it spoke of,[34] God himself has now done what the law could not. This is why Paul states that Christ's death commends God's love (5:8), because it is God himself who has appeared in his flesh to atone for sin.

---

[34] Cf. *"I set before you life and death, blessing and cursing, so choose life"* (Dt. 30:19).

By condemning sin in the body of his son...

It is neither Jesus, nor man, that God condemns on the cross, but man's great enemy – *sin*. That Jesus appears in "the likeness of sinful flesh" (KJV) may refer to the fact that sin, though never belonging to Jesus himself, was judged by God in his flesh.

4. God himself has answered the righteous standard of the law in us.

The Greek wording in this verse implies that what is just in God's sight is now being fulfilled in those who walk by the Spirit. Paul may be referencing the new covenant promises given in Jeremiah and Ezekiel, cf. "I will put my law within them and write it on their hearts" (Jer. 31:33); "I will put a new spirit within you."[35]

Members of the early Church recognized that these and other new covenant promises were now being fulfilled in the Church through the work of the Holy Spirit, cf. "In the last days God says, I will pour out my Spirit on all people" (Joel 2:28).

Who are now walking according to the Spirit, and not the flesh.

To live by the flesh is to live a life which is carnal in its orientation. To live by the Spirit however, is to live under the grace and influence of God himself, resulting in us spontaneously producing the fruit of the Spirit in our own lives.

5. For those who live by the flesh set their minds on the flesh, but those who live by the Spirit set their minds on the Spirit.

Paul here further explores the antitheses between "flesh" and "spirit," cf. "If we live by the Spirit, then we should also walk by the Spirit" (Gal. 5:25). See also Gal. 5:16–17.

---

[35] cf. *"I will put My Spirit within you." (Ezekiel 36:27)*

6. The mind given over to the flesh...the mind given to the Spirit.

Paul's contrast between the mind of the flesh and the mind of the spirit is similar to his contrast between the mind set on "things above" and the mind set on "things of the earth." (Col. 3:2).

Though we are saved, the carnal mind, with its attitudes and perceptions, must still be broken and renewed daily. It is only by learning to think and reason in new ways that our lives are transformed at the behavioral level (cf. Rom. 12:2; Eph. 4:23; Phil. 2:5, 4:8; 2 Cor. 10:5).

9. And if they have not received the Spirit–which is of Christ, then they are not yet his people.

Though Paul has various ways of speaking about the Spirit,[36] it is the singular Spirit of God that is in view. To be "in Christ" (cf. 8:1) is to also be "in the Spirit" (cf. 8:9), and to access one is to access the other. As Matthew Henry wrote: "If the Spirit is in us, then Christ is in us."

10. But if he dwells in you through the Spirit, then the body dies because of sin, but the Spirit lives because of righteousness.

To be made "alive" is to be quickened[37] from death, and everything that shares in its nature or character, i.e., tribulation, hardship, persecution, famine, etc. Paul's meaning here is clear: Though the physical body is still subject to decay; God's Spirit gives life to our spirits through our faith of Jesus.

11. He that raised Christ will also restore life to your bodies through his Spirit, which is now in you as well.

If the body is subject to death because of sin, we must not forget that it too has been given the promise of life by God. Though it is sown in

---

[36] Cf. *"the Spirit of God"* (1 Cor. 2:14), *"the Spirit of Christ"* (Rom. 8:9), *"the Holy Spirit"* (2 Tim. 1:14), *"the Spirit that raised Jesus"* (Rom. 8:11), *"the Spirit of his Son"* (Gal. 4:6), etc.
[37] To *"quicken"* something is to bring it to life, or restore it to a former flourishing condition.

perishability [meaning it *dies*], it will one day rise in imperishability [meaning it will not *die* again].[38]

12. We are therefore in debt, but not to the life of the flesh.

Though the carnal nature is still alive in us, we are no longer under obligation to follow it or honor its desires.

13. To mortify the actions of the flesh—through the life of the Spirit—is to live.

What Paul is teaching in these verses is a way of reasoning about the members of our flesh that lead us to sin, i.e., we are to reckon or consider these physical members as dead or "cut off," just as we are to reckon or consider our hearts circumcised (cf. Dt. 10:16; Jer. 4:4).

14. Those who are now led by God's Spirit are God's children.

When Paul speaks about Christ's people being led to their inheritance by the Spirit he is making a subtle connection between the Church and Israel, who were led in the wilderness by God's Spirit, and Jesus who was led into the wilderness by the Spirit as well (Mk. 1:12–13).

15. His Spirit is not a spirit of bondage, that we should turn in fear; but the Spirit of adoption…

The Exodus of Israel from Egypt was God's primary act of saving grace in the Old Testament. The prophets frequently looked to it as a kind of pattern for the new movement that God would bring about through the Messiah (e.g., Jer. 16:14–15; Micah 7:15).

The concept of adoption in Greek denotes one's election or placement as a son, as opposed to one's natural birth. In the ancient world, an adopted son was deliberately chosen by the adoptive father to perpetuate his name and authority and to inherit his estate. In this sense, the adopted son was not considered inferior in status to the natural son, but at times honored even more so, because they were actually chosen by the father.

---

[38] cf. 1 Cor. 15:42

Augustus, the first emperor of the Roman Empire, Tiberius, Caligula, Nero, Trajan, Hadrian, Antoninus Pius, Marcus Aurelius, and Lucius Verus were each made Emperor of Rome through the peculiar process of adoption.

Abba, Father!

The word "Abba" passed into Hebrew from Aramaic and was the equivalent of the Greek word for father. The two were often combined in the worship of Greek-speaking churches as "Abba, Father," which also appear in Mark 14:36 and Galatians 4:6.

16. His Spirit now witnesses with our spirit that we are his children.

To call God our Father is as much a witness to the Spirit's work within us as it is to call Jesus our Lord, cf. 1 Cor. 12:3.

17. And if we are God's children, then we are also his heirs...

Since the primary purpose of adoption was to provide wealthy persons with a suitable heir, the notion of our adoption leads Paul directly to that of our inheritance.

> Ask of me, and I will give you the nations as your inheritance, and the ends of the earth as your possession. (Psa. 2:8)

If we share in his suffering.

Suffering, for Paul, was an integral part of the Christian story. Though the nature of the suffering may vary from person to person, suffering itself is sure.

> Through suffering our bodies continue to share in the dying of Jesus so that his life may be seen in us as well. (2 Cor. 4:10)

18. Our present sufferings are of no comparison with the coming glory which shall be revealed in us.

By "suffering," Paul means our affliction or pain in the present. While this suffering is temporal and passing, the glory being revealed in us as a result is eternal.

20. Subjected to the curse of futility.

Because of Adam's sin creation was made subject to "vanity" or "frustration," cf. "Cursed is the ground because of you" (Gen. 3:17). Though blameless, the earth itself has been robed in futility until its redemption.

The Greek word for "vanity" also suggests the worship of false gods or powers, as in Acts 14:15, and may imply that creation has been enslaved to malignant forces (1 Cor. 12:2), cf. "The god of this world has blinded their minds" (2 Cor. 4:4).

21. Creation too is going to be loosed from its enslavement to decay.

Creation does not presently exist in the state in which it was first constituted.[39] Though its physical elements are intact, the major effect of its corruption has been the moral and spiritual decay in which it presently groans. From the perspective of Genesis the physical creation as it stands is no longer *tōv*, meaning "good," but *rah*, meaning "evil" or "corrupted."

The freedom revealed when God's children are finally glorified.

Paul's words can literally be translated as "the glorious freedom" or "the freedom of glory." Either way, man is here presented as a kind of first fruit for whose redemption creation waits with earnest expectation.

> He gave us birth through the word of truth, that we might
> be a kind of firstfruits of all that he created. (James 1:18)

---

[39] Cf. Gen. 1:31, where all that has been made is looked upon by God and called *tōv* (*"good"*), which means *well-formed, agreeable, without blemish or taint*, i.e., *without sin*.

22. Creation is travailing, even now, as if it were in labor.

Paul here draws a subtle connection between the travailing of creation and the state of Eve, our first mother, after the Fall, cf. "In travail you will bring forth children" (Gen. 3:16).

Like Eve, creation has been subjected to travail, or what Jesus called "the beginnings of birth pains" (Mk. 13:7). These pains include earthquakes, famines, persecution, and even wars (Mk. 13:7–8).

In Judaism, the travail leading to the coming of Messiah is called "the birth pains of Messiah." For Paul, these pains were not simply a future reality, but were already present in the world because of sin.

23. The first fruit of the Spirit's life within us.

First fruit is a harvest metaphor and reflects the command for Israel to present the first portion of their grain and new wine as a seasonal offering to God (cf. Exod. 23:19; Lev. 23:10; Num. 28:26; 2 Chron. 31:5). This offering was a visible token of Israel's obedience, as well as their faith that the larger harvest would soon follow its initial fruits.

For Paul, the work of the indwelling Spirit was like the first fruit of the coming harvest. What the believers experienced through the Spirit was the beginning signs of their later salvation.[40]

24–25. For such is the hope of salvation.

The phrase "we were saved" implies that salvation has already happened, and yet the word hope implies that it is in some ways still future. Paul is reminding his readers that salvation in the present is a matter of one's faith, while the fulness of the coming resurrection remains a future reality for which we are still waiting in expectant hope.

---

[40] Cf. 2 Cor. 1:22; 5:5; and Eph. 1:14, where the Spirit is described as an *arrabōn*, meaning a down payment or pledge against the coming salvation which was still future.

26. The Spirit is now joined with us—helping us in our weaknesses...

As our advocate or counselor, the Spirit joins with us in our weakness and intercedes on our behalf with the Father. While Christ is seated at the right hand of God making intercession for the saints, the intercession of the Spirit is presented by Paul as taking place within the personal being of the believers themselves.

With sighing deeper than our own words...

The deep sighing or groanings in v. 26 belong to the Spirit and not the believer. It is the Spirit who leads us in prayer, whether we pray with tongues or our understanding. Because of this, God's power is often brought to bear in the midst of situations we may still be unaware of.

28. We know that God is bringing all things together for the good of those who love him.

The words "we know" express the assurance we have of God's sovereignty over all things, cf. "over every event of life" (Alford, 1884).

Everything, Paul says, *even tragedy*, is being brought together by God for the outworking of what he calls "good."

Those who are called according to his purpose.

For Paul, the idea of being "called" was tantamount to being drawn by the Spirit, cf. "the calling to which you were called" (Eph. 4:1), "who called you out of darkness" (1 Pet. 2:9), "called to be saints" (Rom. 1:7).

It is the effectual calling of God – *through the Spirit* – that draws us into relationship with Jesus (cf. John 6:44). To be "called" does not mean "politely invited," but "pulled" or "carried" by God himself.

29. For whom he foreknew, he also predestined...

By "foreknew," Paul is not simply referring to God's knowing, but to his election as well, cf. "Before I formed you in the womb I knew you...I set you apart...I appointed you" (Jer. 1:5); "You didn't choose me, but I chose you" (Jn. 15:16).

30. He also called...declared just...glorified.

Paul's emphasis here is on God's unfailing commitment to bring to glory every person declared righteous through personal faith in Jesus.

32. He did not withhold his own son...

There is an unmistakable echo of the binding of Isaac from Genesis 22 in the present verse. In the narrative, God commands Abraham to sacrifice his son Isaac. In the gospel however, it is God, and not man, who becomes the willing father of the sacrifice. In this sense, Abraham, by offering up his son, foreshadows the role of God himself.

33-34. Who then can accuse God's elect?

Paul may here have in mind the Satan[41] or other lesser accusers who bring accusations before God against his people (Rev. 12:10).

> Then he showed me Yeshūah the high priest standing before the angel of Yahweh, and the Satan standing at his right side to accuse him. (Zech. 3:1)

Seated at the right hand of God...

> Yahweh said unto my Lord: Sit at My right hand until I make your enemies a footstool beneath you. (Psa. 110:1)

From the earliest days of the church, Psalm 110 was read as a Messianic psalm, referencing the role of Jesus (cf. Matt. 22:41–45; Acts 2:32–36). Paul echoes it in other places as well:

---

[41] The word "satan" is not a proper name but a title which appears in the Hebrew and the Greek with the definite article in front of it. *Ha-satan* ("the satan") in Hebrew refers to "one who stands against" or "opposes" another. Though most commonly used to denote the spiritual being who accuses others before God (Job 1:6; 2:1; and Zech. 3:1), the title is also given to humans who oppose one another (1 Kings 5:4; 11:14, 23), as well as the angel of Yahweh (Numbers 22:22).

He raised him from the dead and set him at his right
hand...and hath put all things under his feet...[42]

Interceding for us.

In Jesus' intercession for the church there is an echo of the fourth Servant
Song as well (cf. Isa. 52:13–53:12). "He bore the sin of many and made
intercession for the transgressors" (Isa. 53:12).

The intercession of Christ before God is a priestly function. As the writer
of Hebrews notes: "He lives forever to intercede with God on their behalf"
(Heb. 7:25).

36. For your sake we are being killed all day long...

Paul here draws from Psalm 44:22, where Israel is depicted as suffering
for their fidelity to God, as were many of the saints in the early church (cf.
Acts 5:41; 1 Pet. 2:21; 4:15–19).

37. But even in these...

The juxtaposition of suffering and glory in faith are once more held in
view by Paul. *We are being killed,* he writes, *and counted as sheep for the
slaughter* (8:36); *but even in these we are prevailing and conquering as God's
people.*

**38–39. Neither death nor life, angels or principalities, things present or
things to come...**

No power or force, no behavior, no action (on our part or others), no span
of time, nor things imaginable (or unimaginable) can separate Christ's
people from the love of God revealed in Jesus. This is the concluding point
of Romans 8.

---

[42] Eph. 1:19–22, see also Lk. 22:69; Acts 5:31; Heb. 8:1; 10:12; 12:2; 1 Pet. 3:22.

X

THE CHILDREN
OF ABRAHAM

Romans 9:1–29

9 I am telling you the truth in Christ and not exaggerating the facts. My own conscience bears witness in the Holy Spirit [2] of how deeply I have grieved [3] for my people according to the flesh. I almost wish that I could be accursed, or even cut off from Christ, if it would save [4] those descended from Israel. For they are the ones to whom the adoption, glory, and covenants were first given, as well as the Law, the right of service, and the promises. [5] They are the sons of the fathers; and the ones to whom Christ was born according to the flesh—who is God over all and blessed forever. Amen.

[6] So what should we say now? That God's word to Israel has failed? No! For they are not all "Israel" just because they came out of Israel; [7] nor is every child born of Abraham counted as his seed. For it says, through Isaac shall your seed be called. [8] So the children of natural descent were not all counted as the children of God, but the children of the promise were. It is they who are regarded by God as Abraham's seed. [9] And this is the word given by promise: At this time I will come, and Sarah shall have a son.

[10] The same thing happened when Rebekah conceived children by our father Isaac. [11] Before the children were born or had done anything right or wrong, it was said to her, the older will serve the younger. It happened this way so that God's purpose according to election might stand, and that it would not be considered a matter of works, but of God's calling. [13] And it was written afterward, Jacob I loved, but Esau I esteemed not. [14] What then? Is God unjust in the way he deals with man?

No! [15] For he says to Moses, I have mercy on whom I have mercy, and compassion on whom I have compassion.

[16] So it is not a matter of willingness or effort, but of God's mercy. [17] For the scripture says concerning Pharaoh: For this reason, I raised you up, that I might show my power in you, and that my name might be declared throughout the earth. [18] So God has mercy on whom he wills, and whom he wills, he hardens.

[19] Well then, you ask, why does he still find fault with us? For who has resisted his will? [20] But who are you, o man, to question God? Does the clay question the hand of the potter saying why did you shape me this way? [21] Or is it not the potter that exercises authority and will over the clay? Can the potter not make vessels for honor and dishonor from the same lump? [22] Supposing God desired to show his power in the present. What if he endured the vessels of ruin [23] in order to reveal his glory on the vessels of mercy, [24] both Jews and non-Jews predestined for glory. [25] For he says in Hosea,

> I will call those who were not my people, my people, and her who was not beloved, my beloved. [26] And in the place where it was said to them, you are not my people, there they shall be called the children of the living God.

[27] Isaiah also cries out to his nation,

> Though the number of Israel's sons are like the sand of the sea, only a remnant shall be saved; [28] for the LORD will execute his word on the earth, both thoroughly and quickly.

[29] And in another place it is written,

> Unless the LORD of Sabaoth had left us a seed, we would have become as desolate as Sodom and Gomorrah.

[30] What more shall we say? That the nations who were not pursuing righteousness have found it, and have now been made right with God by faith? [31] And that Israel, who pursued righteousness by the very law that God prescribed, have not? [32] But why, you ask? Because they sought it by the merit of their own works and not by faith in God himself; and stumbled over the stumbling stone, [33] just as it was written:

> Behold, I lay in Zion a stone which shall cause stumbling, and a rock that shall offend; but he that has faith in him shall not suffer shame.

The problem that Paul takes up in chapters 9–11, is one with which he has wrestled since coming to the Lord, i.e., the refusal of Israel to accept the salvation proclaimed through her Messiah, even while those who are not ethnically Jewish are embracing it in large numbers.

1. My own conscience bears witness in the Holy Spirit

While the Spirit of God bore witness to Paul's love for his nation, his inner conscience also bore witness to his deep love as well. For a fuller explanation of Paul's use of the word "conscience" see the note on Romans 2:15.

3. I almost wish that I could be accursed, or even cut off from Christ...

To be accursed literally meant to be made an offering or given up, while "cut off" adds the idea of separation or removal from Jesus himself. There is an unmistakable echo here of Moses' prayer for Israel:

> If you will not forgive their sin, then strike me also from the book you have written.[43]

The kinsmen to whom Paul refers are his racial brethren, meaning his brothers according to the flesh. Despite his mission to the Gentiles, Paul never ceased to identify himself as a racial or ethnic Jew, cf. "I am a Jew" (Acts 22:3), "I too am an Israelite" (Romans 11:1).

4. They are the ones to whom the adoption, glory, and covenants were first given, as well as the Law, the right of service, and the promises.

The Greek word for adoption literally meant one's placement as a son,[44] while glory pertained to God's visible presence among his people. The covenants, though variously numbered, likely included several repetitions of God's covenant with Abraham, and the right of service pertained to the ordinances of the Temple.

---

[43] Exodus 32:32
[44] "Thus saith the LORD, Israel *is* my son, *even* my firstborn." (Ex. 4:22, KJV)

5. The ones to whom Christ was born according to the flesh.

Israel's preeminence is here summed up in its relation to its Messiah, who is above all, and blessed of God forever.

6. So what should we say now? That God's word to Israel has failed?

If national Israel has turned away from God's plan to use them as a light for other nations and the people of the Messiah, then it would seem fair to say that the plan itself had failed, fallen off course, or been without effect.

Paul's response to this line of reasoning is an emphatic "No!" For they are not truly "Israel" simply because they descend from Jacob. Nor is every physical descendant of Abraham counted as his seed, but those rather who continue in his faith, cf. "If you were Abraham's children, then you would do what Abraham did" (Jn. 8:39).

7. Through Isaac shall your seed be called,

By God's own election Abraham's seed was to be numbered through Isaac, and not the other sons born to him through Hagar and Keturah.[45]

Paul also uses Isaac, Jacob (vv. 10–13), and Pharaoh (vv. 14–18) as further examples of God's sovereignty and election.

8. So the children of natural descent were not all counted as the children of God, but the children of the promise were.

When God spoke of Abraham's seed it was not a reference to every physical descendent born in his line, but to those born according to his promise: "At this time I will come and Sarah shall have a son" (9:9).

11. That it would not be considered a matter of works, but of God's calling.

Cf. "called of Jesus" (1:6), "called to be saints" (1:7), "called according to his purpose" (8:28).

---

[45] Cf. "Abraham took another wife whose name was Keturah. She bore him Zimran, and Jokshan, and Medan, and Midian, and Ishbak, and Shuah" (Gen. 25:1–2, KJV).

12. The older will serve the younger.

In vv. 12-13, the names "Jacob" and "Esau" refer to nations, and not individuals, cf. "Two nations are in your womb" (Gen. 25:23). Historically, Esau never served Jacob, and though Jacob prospered, he was never considered the stronger.

It was Esau's descendants as well, and not Esau, who God judged for rejoicing over Jerusalem's destruction, and Esau descendants who served the descendants of Jacob, *cf. the older shall serve the younger.*

> I will take vengeance on Edom by the hand of my people
> Israel, and they will deal with Edom according to my
> wrath. (Ez. 25:14)[46]

13. Jacob I loved, but Esau I esteemed not.

That Jacob is never depicted as a person of exceptional character demonstrates that God's election was not based on the personal merit of the elected, but on the divine will and purposes of God himself.

15. I have mercy on whom I have mercy, and compassion on whom I have compassion.

Paul shows from Exodus 33:19, that even God's mercy is a matter of his election. Since all people sin, his choice of one over the other is never unjust, but an act of his mercy towards the one chosen.

16. So it is not a matter of willingness or effort, but of God's mercy.

Paul here contrasts our will and effort with the mercy by which God calls us for his own purposes.

17. The scripture says concerning Pharaoh...

The Pharaoh mentioned here is the Pharaoh of the Exodus, and not the Pharaoh of the oppression whose death is recorded in Ex. 2:23.

---

[46] Cf. 2 Sam. 8:14; 1 Kings 22:47; 2 Kings 14:7.

For this reason, I raised you up.

The inference here may be that God created Pharaoh and then raised him up, or that God sustained him on the throne for an appointed time, cf. "for this reason I have allowed you to remain" (NASB); "I have spared you for a purpose" (NLT).

That my name might be declared throughout the earth.

For further proof of the manner in which the Exodus caused God's name to be spread among the nations, see: Josh. 2:10–11; 9:9; and 1 Sam. 4:8.

> The nations have heard; they tremble; dread has seized the inhabitants of Philistia. The chiefs of Edom are in terror; the nobles of Moab tremble; and the strength of Canaan has vanished.[47]

18. God has mercy on whom he wills, and whom he wills, he hardens.

There is much debate concerning the Old Testament verses to which Paul here alludes. In them God is said to be the one who actually "hardens" the heart of Pharaoh (cf. Ex. 4:21; 7:3; 9:12; 14:4).

It should be noted that God is nowhere in Scripture said to harden the heart of anyone who had not first hardened themselves. One might also consider Romans 1, where the phrase "God gave them over" appears three times as a referent for God handing man over to the very sin he has already demanded (1:24; 1:26; 1:28).

It is best not to be overly dogmatic here, seeing as Paul's purpose in writing was not to explain God's sovereign right to harden the heart of a despot, but to make sense of the hardening which had taken hold of Israel.

> The reconciliation of God's sovereignty and man's responsibility is beyond our power. The Bible states and emphasizes both, and then leaves them. We shall be wise if we do the same. – Thomas, G.

---

[47] Exodus 15:14-15

20. Does the clay question the hand of the potter...

"Does the clay say to the one who forms it, what are you making?" (Isa. 45:9); "Can the pottery say of the potter, he does not understand?" (Isa. 29:16)

21. Vessels for honor and dishonor from the same lump.

In a great house there are not only vessels of gold and silver, but also wooden and earthen; and some indeed are unto honor, but some unto dishonor. (2 Tim. 2:20)

25. I will call those who were not my people, my people, and her who was not beloved, my beloved.

These words from Hosea 2:23, were originally a promise of covenant renewal for Israel, not Gentiles.[48] The promise inferred that those who had been scattered in judgment for breaking God's covenant would be brought back to the land by God himself.

In 1 Pet. 2:10, Peter applies the restoration promise of Hosea to the entire Jewish + Gentile church. Where it was once said of dispersed Jews and Gentiles alike, "you are not my people," it was now being said of them both, "you are the children of the living God."

27. Only a remnant shall be saved.

Isaiah had prophesied that only a remnant would return from exile, and that in returning they would also be turning back to God himself (cf. Isa. 10:21).

As a witness to this Isaiah named his oldest son *She-ār yāshūb*, meaning "a remnant will return" (Is. 7:3; 8:18). For Paul, the returning remnant were the believing Jews who had embraced Jesus as their Messiah.

His points in the previous section can be summarized as follows:

[1] Not all ethnic Jews were counted as "Israel" (vv. 6–8).
[2] Not all ethnic Jews were chosen by God (v. 24).

---

[48] Cf. 1 Pet. 2:10, where Peter applies this promise to the entire Jewish/Gentile church.

[3] Not all those chosen by God were ethnically Jewish (v. 24).

28. The LORD will execute his word on the earth, both thoroughly and quickly.

Paul here draws from Isaiah 10:23, where God himself has vowed to bring about a fulfillment of his word in the earth.

29. Unless the LORD of Sabaoth had left us a seed...

Paul here quotes from Isaiah 1:9, where the remnant spoken of were the racial descendants of Jacob who had remained faithful to God's covenant after Assyrian invasion.

If God had not tempered his judgment with mercy, he would have destroyed Israel as completely as he had destroyed other nations. This remnant of believing descendants among racial Jews was further proof of God's continued mercy upon Israel's sons and daughters.

XI

COVENANT FAITHFULNESS

Romans 9:30–10:21

[30] So what shall we say? That those who were not pursuing righteousness have found it by faith? [31] And that Israel, who pursued it by the law of God have not? [32] But why? Because they sought it by the merit of their own works and not by their faith in God himself; and stumbled over the stumbling stone, [33] just as it was written:

> Behold, I lay in Zion a stone which shall cause stumbling, and
> a rock that shall offend; but he that has faith in him shall not
> be put to shame.

10 Brothers, it is my heart's desire and prayer to God that Israel be saved, [2] for I know they are zealous for the things of God. The problem is that their zeal is not based on *knowing*, [3] for they have misunderstood the righteousness of God and worked to establish a righteousness of their own. Because of this, they have failed to grasp the righteousness that comes from God alone. [4] For the coming of Christ was the true end of the law, that righteousness might come to all that have faith.

[5] Moses testifies about the righteousness of the law, saying: the person who keeps these things shall live by them. [6] But concerning the righteousness of faith, he says: Do not say in your heart, who shall ascend into heaven? (as if to bring Christ down), [7] or who shall descend into the depths? (as if to raise him up). [8] But what does it say? The word is close at hand; it is on your lips and in your heart, meaning the word of faith. [9] If you then confess with your mouth that Jesus is Lord and have faith in your heart that God raised him from the dead, you will be saved. [10] Why? Because it is in the heart that faith is held unto righteousness; and with the mouth

that confession is made unto salvation. [11] For the scripture says, he that has faith in him shall not be put to shame. [12] There is no difference here between the Jew and the Greek, seeing as it is the same Lord who reigns over all, and is rich toward all who call on him. [13] For all who call upon the name of the LORD shall be saved.

[14] But how will they call on him if they have not had faith? And how will they have faith if they have not heard? And how will they hear if he is not announced? [15] And how will the announcement be made if no one is sent to make it? For as it is written, how beautiful are the feet of those who bring good tidings of good things!

[16] But not everyone has obeyed the good news, just as Isaiah states, LORD, who has believed our report? [17] So then, faith comes by hearing, and hearing by the word of Christ. [18] But one might ask, have they not heard the word? Yes! They have heard it, for the scripture says: Their voices went out into all the earth, and their words to the ends of the world.

[19] But what about Israel? Did they not know? Yes, they knew. For even in the time of Moses God says, I will rouse you to jealousy using those who are not a people and provoke you to anger with a nation that has no understanding.

[20] Isaiah too speaks boldly for God, saying, I was found by those who were not seeking me; and revealed myself to them who did not ask for me.

[21] But concerning Israel, he says, All day long have I stretched out my hands to a disbelieving and disobedient people.

Paul now takes up the subject of Israel's stumbling. The point which he arrives at is that Israel's stumbling was foreseen by God and was now being used by him to further his own purposes, which include the establishment of a single multiethnic family united by faith in Christ.

31. [they] pursued it by the law of God.

Some Jews held that keeping the law was the only way of being made right with God. The problem is that by focusing solely on the law's outer form many were missing its true spirit and intent altogether.

32. [they] stumbled over the stumbling stone.

God says through Isaiah that he is a sanctuary or holy place for those who trust in him, and a stone of stumbling for those who trust in anything else (cf. Isa. 8:14).

33. Behold, I lay in Zion a stone which shall cause stumbling, and a rock that shall offend.

This stone has been variously understood as a referent for God, the remnant in Israel, or the Messiah. In the New Testament, Jesus is the divinely laid stone who becomes a refuge for people of faith and an offense for others.

2. I know they are zealous for the things of God.

Paul knew from his own experiences what it meant to be zealous for God, and yet ignorant of what God himself was doing in and through Christ. He reminds us elsewhere that just as Israel now disparaged the name of Jesus (cf. Acts 4:18; 5:40), he too had once blasphemed against him as well (1 Tim. 1:13).

3. They have misunderstood the righteousness of God.

Some of Christ's early followers insisted that non-Jewish Christians undergo formal conversion to Judaism if they hoped to be justified. Paul's answer was a far simpler one: Men and women are justified by faith alone!

4. For the coming of Christ was the true end of the law.

If the aim of the Law was to make men right with God, then the end of the Law is Jesus, cf. "I did not come to abolish the law or the prophets, but to accomplish their purpose" (Matt. 5:17).

5. The person who keeps these things shall live by them.

In order to be satisfied the Law required an actual fulfilment of its commands. Its essence was found in our works and obedience, not our faith.

6. Do not say in your heart, who shall ascend into heaven...

Paul warns against reasoning in a way that undermines Christ's coming from above or resurrection. Perfect faith, he insists, reasons in the following manner: "Do not try to climb the heavens or search the depths for Jesus. He has already come down from heaven to earth, been crucified, buried, and raised, and is now risen back to heaven. He is yours through faith right where you are."

9. Confess with your mouth that Jesus is Lord and have faith in your heart that God raised him from the dead...

Our confession that Jesus is Lord is rooted in our belief that God raised him from the dead. He is only Lord because he now lives.

The word translated "confess" means to speak the same word. The believer's mouth and heart must come into agreement in matters of faith and confess the same things with respect to Christ.

10. Because it is in the heart that faith is held unto righteousness; and with the mouth that confession is made unto salvation.

Both faith (believing) and confession are eschatological in the sense that they connect us in the present to the future reality of our salvation in Christ.

11. He that has faith in him shall not be put to shame.

Quoted from Isaiah 28:16 (see also 9:33).

12. There is no difference here between the Jew and the Greek.

Since faith alone gives us access to God, it is faith alone to which his grace responds, making no distinction between the race or ethnic descent of the one having faith.

13. All who call upon the name of the LORD shall be saved.

Paul is here quoting from Joel 2:32, where the word "LORD" is actually "Yahweh" in Hebrew. In referring to Jesus as the LORD of Joel's prophecy,

Paul is not only declaring his kingship over the earth but equating him with Yahweh the covenant God of Israel as well.

14. How will they call on him if they have not had faith?

Paul here connects salvation (calling on God) with faith, and faith with hearing the word of Christ. Hearing of course, requires that a word is first proclaimed, and this likewise requires that someone be sent to proclaim it.

As followers of Jesus, we have all been given the authority to proclaim the gospel to the lost, and to make disciples of those who come to faith (Matt. 28:19–20). In this way we are all, without exception, called and sent out as ambassadors of Christ.

16. LORD, who has believed our report?

This question, taken from Isaiah 53:1, is being asked by those bearing witness to the vindication of God's Servant. In the Servant Songs of Isaiah, the Arm of the LORD who saves and the Servant of the LORD who suffers are revealed to be one and the same, leaving the prophet to ask, "Who has believed our report? And to whom has the arm of the LORD been revealed?" (Isaiah 53.1).

17. So then, faith comes by hearing…

Faith begins with hearing a faith-producing word and is an inward conviction that what one has heard is true. By "hearing the word of Christ," Paul means the word proclaimed about Jesus, which is the same word that awakens faith in those who hear.

18. Their voices went out into all the earth, and their words to the ends of the world.

These words from Psalm 19:4, originally referred to the universal witness of the constellations. Just as every human had access to the witness of nature (cf. 1:19–20), so nearly all Jews had access to the witness of Jesus.

19. I will rouse you to jealousy using those who are not a people...

Because Israel had moved God to jealousy by worshipping what was not truly god, Paul states that he has now moved them to jealousy by blessing those who were not truly a people (cf. Deut. 32:21).

20. I was found by those who were not seeking me; and revealed myself to them who did not ask for me.

Though the verses Paul is quoting from Isaiah refer to the rebelliousness of Israel, Paul is using them as a referent for both non-Jews and Jews alike.

> I allowed myself to be sought by those who were not asking for me; and to be found by those who did not seek me. To a nation that was not called by my name I said, "Here I am, here I am." (Isa. 65:1)

21. All day long have I stretched out my hands to a disbelieving and disobedient people.

These words from Isaiah 65:2 were as true of Paul's contemporaries as they had been of Isaiah's. Paul finds in them an apt description of the Jews who were unwilling to receive God's outstretched hand, which had now been extended through the hand of Jesus.

XII

THE REMNANT

Romans 11:1–36

11 What then, has God abandoned his people? No! For I too am an Israelite, descended from Abraham through the tribe of Benjamin. ² God has not abandoned his people who he foreknew. Or have you not read in the Scriptures how Elijah pleads against Israel, saying, ³ "Lord, they have killed your prophets, and torn down your altars, and I alone am left, and they are now seeking my life."

⁴ But how does God answer him? "I have set apart for myself seven thousand men who have not bowed the knee to Baal."

⁵ So even now, God has a remnant set apart by grace. ⁶ And if they are set apart by grace, then it is no longer a matter of personal works: otherwise grace is no longer grace.

⁷ So Israel has not found what it sought; though those set apart by grace have. The rest have been hardened. ⁸ Just as it was written: "God gave them over to a spirit of slumber, and to eyes that do not see, and to ears that do not hear; and it has remained so unto this day."

⁹ Even David says of them: "May their table be made a snare and a trap, and a cause of stumbling, and retribution: ¹⁰ And may their eyes be darkened so as not to see, and their backs bent always."

¹¹ But have they stumbled to the point of falling away? No! But through their trespass, salvation has come to the nations, and they themselves provoked to jealousy. ¹² And if their trespass and loss has brought gain to the world and the nations; how much more will their fullness bring with it?

¹³ I am speaking to those of you who are Gentiles. Because I am an apostle to other nations, I boast in my ministry to you, ¹⁴ that in doing so I might provoke my own people to jealousy and perhaps save some. ¹⁵ For if their loss means reconciliation for the world, what more will their gain mean, but life from the dead?

¹⁶ And if the first fruits are holy, then the dough is holy also; and if the root is holy, then the branches are holy too. ¹⁷ Now if natural branches were broken off so that you, who were uncultivated branches, could be grafted in among them to share in the root and fatness of the olive, ¹⁸ then do not boast over the severed branches. If you have boasted, then remember that it is not you who bears the root, but the root that bears you.

¹⁹ Now you may say that the branches were broken off so that you could be grafted in. ²⁰ Yes, but they were only broken off because of unfaith, and you have only stood because of faith. So, do not boast over them, but be reverent: ²¹ After all, if God didn't spare the natural branches, how much more might he cast off the unnatural.

²² For there is both grace and severity with God: severity upon those who fell, but grace upon you who stand; that is—if you continue in his grace. Otherwise, you too may be cut off. ²³ And if they turn from their unfaith, then they too may be grafted back in, for God is able to restore them. ²⁴ If you being uncultivated were grafted into the olive tree, how much more can the natural branches of that tree be grafted into their former place?

²⁵ Now brethren, I don't want you to be ignorant of this mystery, or arrogant. Israel has been hardened, but only until the nations have fully entered in. ²⁶ For this is how all Israel shall be saved, even as the scripture says:

> The Deliverer shall come out of Zion and remove ungodliness
> from Jacob. ²⁷ And my covenant with them shall be that I remove
> their sins.

²⁸ With regard to the good news, some are enemies for your sake! But with regard to election, some are loved for the sake of the fathers, ²⁹ for God's grace and calling are not undone. ³⁰ Just as you were once without faith and found mercy through the unbelief of others, ³¹ so others are now without faith, and may find mercy through the mercy given to you. ³² For God has proven that all have been without faith, that he might also show that all have received mercy. ³³ How vast is the richness of his wisdom and knowing! And how far beyond our understanding are his judgments!

³⁴ For who of us has known the mind of the LORD, or given him counsel? ³⁵ Or first given to him, that it should afterward be repaid to them?

³⁶ From him, through him, and unto him are all things! And to him alone is glory unto the ages. Amen.

1. I too am an Israelite, descended from Abraham through the tribe of Benjamin.

In recounting Israel's history, Paul has been reconciling the nation's election with their present unbelief. Even Israel's stumbling was in keeping with the sovereign purposes of God, who had reserved for himself a "remnant" of believing Jews according to his own election.

Paul's first proof against the idea of Jewish abandonment was the fact that he himself was a descendant of Abraham and a Benjamite, and therefore evidence of a believing remnant of Jews in Christ.

4. I have set apart for myself seven thousand men who have not bowed the knee to Baal.

Paul uses Elijah's plea against Israel, quoted from 1 Kings 19:10, 14, to demonstrate God's pattern in setting apart a remnant of believing Jews in Christ.

7. The rest have been hardened.

Those who were not called were hardened, or unrepentant before God. This hardening is variously described by Paul, as well as the Hebrew prophets, as a kind of blindness, deafness, or sleep.

> The LORD has poured out a spirit of sleep upon you and closed your eyes so that you no longer see. (Isa. 29:10)

9. May their table be made a snare and a trap, and a cause of stumbling, and retribution…

These verses reference David's prayer in the Psalms that his enemy's comfort and blessings would become a cause of stumbling for them.

11. Have they stumbled to the point of falling away? No! But through their trespass, salvation has come to the nations...

A peculiar characteristic of Israel's fall is that it has had redemptive consequences for the world. Firstly, in handing Christ over to Roman powers, Israel had merely carried out what God had already purposed (cf. Acts 4:28). Secondly, for Paul, it is the Jewish rejection of Christ that often leads directly to the gospelizing of the Gentiles:

> And when they opposed and reviled him, he shook out his garments and said to them, "Your blood be on your own heads! I am innocent. From now on I will go to the Gentiles." (Acts 18:6, ESV)

15. For if their loss means reconciliation for the world, what more will their gain mean, but life from the dead?

The words *life from the dead* are likely figurative, signifying the coming of life to those presently in a state of death, cf. "I will put my Spirit in you, and you will live" (Ezek. 37:14). Paul may also be suggesting that the future restoration of the Jews will bring about a revival of faith in others.

16. If the first fruits are holy, then the dough is holy also; and if the root is holy, then the branches are holy too.

Paul's point is that later Jewish believers will share in the holiness of the earlier believers who embraced Israel's Messiah when he came. If these Jewish believers, like Paul and the apostles, are the first fruits, then the latter "lump" (NASB) are the Jewish believers who will eventually follow in faith.

The root and branches in Paul's second image are variously interpreted, though the principle is identical. As life flows from the root to the branches, so holiness and love flow to the sons and daughters for the sake of the fathers (v. 28).

17. Natural branches were broken off so that you, who were uncultivated branches, could be grafted in among them...

Proselytes to the Jewish faith were often spoken of as wild branches grafted on to the olive tree of Israel. For his part, Paul never refers to non-Jews being grafted onto Israel itself. Instead, Gentiles are said to be grafted in among them, and made partakers of the root and fatness of the olive, which may be Abraham, the fathers, God, or even Jesus.

20. They were only broken off because of unfaith, and you have only stood because of faith.

Jews and non-Jews alike are established by faith, and not human merit or works, leaving no one an opportunity to boast (Eph. 2:8–9).

22. That is–if you continue in his grace.

While Scripture affirms God's power to uphold us indefinitely, it also affirms our personal responsibility to continue in his grace.

The two sides are often pitted against one another, as if God's ability to hold us up relieves us of our responsibility to continue standing ourselves. The Bible, however, affirms both.

24. How much more can the natural branches of that tree be grafted into their former place?

If God has grafted unnatural branches onto the olive tree, then it should not be difficult to imagine the natural branches of that tree, in this case ethnic Israel, being grafted back on as well.

25. I don't want you to be ignorant of this mystery, or arrogant.

That all Israel would be saved, despite its present hardening, was a new revelation being given to the church through Paul.

Israel has been hardened, but only until the nations have fully entered in.

The words fully entered in refer to the full number of Gentiles that will be saved according to election. The fullness of their entering in, Paul states, will be followed by the fullness of Israel (v. 12).

26. For this is how all Israel shall be saved…

The phrase "all Israel" may imply "national Israel as a whole," though it should be remembered that for Paul not every person who was ethnically and culturally Jewish was an "Israelite" in the truer sense (cf. Rom. 9:6).

It should also be noted that Paul has already expanded the meaning of words such as *Jew, circumcision,* and *Israel,* so that they now include both Jews and Gentiles being brought to life through faith in Christ (cf. Rom. 2:29; Phil. 3:3; Gal. 6:16).

The Deliverer shall come out of Zion and remove ungodliness from Jacob.

Quoted from Isaiah 59:20, where the reference is to the manifestation of Israel's redeemer in Zion, or for Zion's sake (LXX).

27. And my covenant with them shall be that I remove their sins.

Paul here combines words taken from Isaiah 59 and 27, and Jeremiah 31, which each extend the New Covenant promise of forgiveness to Israel.

28. With regard to the good news, some are enemies for your sake!

Paul states that Israel may have been hardened to the gospel, but only for the sake of those who were now being saved by it (cf. Acts 18:5–6).

With regard to election, some are loved for the sake of the fathers,

The promises made to the fathers are secured to those of their offspring who not only descend from them physically, but walk in their actual steps as well, cf. "If ye were truly Abraham's children, then you would do what Abraham did." (John 8:39).

32. That he might also show that all have received mercy.

Paul argues that God was not obligated to bless one group of people over another, not even the Jews, seeing as all were equally under sin, and equally in need of the mercy offered to them in Christ.

33. How vast is the richness of his wisdom and knowing.

Paul concludes what has been said up to this point with a spontaneous praise of God's wisdom and knowing. This statement has been treated by some as an affirmation of three separate divine qualities, i.e., the richness and wisdom and knowing of God.

34. Who of us has known the mind of the LORD, or given him counsel?

Cf. "Who has directed the Spirit of the LORD, or instructed him as his counselor?" (Isaiah 40:13)

35. Or first given to him, that it should afterward be repaid to them?

Cf. "Who has first given to me, that I should afterward repay him?" (Job 41:11)

36. From him, through him, and unto him, are all things! And to him alone is glory unto the ages.

Whatever exists in heaven or earth is *from* God—the fount of all creation, *through* God—the Word[49] of all creation, and *to* God—the *end* of all creation. To him alone is glory unto the ages.

---

[49] Cf. "Through him all things were made; and without him nothing was made that has been made (John 1:3).

XIII

LIVING SACRIFICES

Romans 12:1–21

12 Brothers, I am appealing to you because of God's mercy in your lives, that you offer your bodies up as living sacrifices made holy and acceptable to God. Such is our reasonable worship. ² And do not conform yourselves to the world around you, but be transformed by the renewing of your minds, working out the will of God, and what is good, pleasing, and acceptable, in your own lives.

³ I speak through the grace given to me by God, that you not think more highly of yourselves than God has raised you. But be sober-minded, regarding yourselves after the measure of faith given to each of you. ⁴ For just as a single body has different limbs with different functions: ⁵ so it is with the body of Christ. We too, having many limbs with different functions, are each joined to the other as one body in Christ.

⁶ And having our unique gifts, we each serve according to the grace given to us. If we prophecy, then we prophecy according to our faith, ⁷ and if we minister, then we minister according to our faith. If we teach, then we teach, ⁸ and if we exhort, then we exhort; but each according to the faith they have received from God. As we give let us not be double-minded; as we lead, then let us lead with energy; and if we show mercy, then let us do so with cheerfulness.

⁹ Love must be unfeigned. So hate what is evil and hold to what is good.¹⁰ Love one another as family; and esteem one another in honor. ¹¹ Do not be lazy in serving the Lord but be lit with the spirit. ¹² Celebrate your hope; enduring tribulation; and giving constant energy to prayer; ¹³ sharing in the needs of God's people; and showing love to the stranger.

¹⁴Speak blessings on those who persecute you; blessings and not cursing. ¹⁵Rejoice with those who rejoice and mourn with those who mourn. ¹⁶Be like minded with one another, not puffed up, but a companion of the lowly. And do not think yourselves wise in your own sight.

¹⁷Do not return evil to others but take thought to what is right and just. ¹⁸If it is possible—as much as it is in your power—live peaceably with all people.

¹⁹Beloved, do not avenge yourselves against one another, but give place to God's wrath: for it is written, It is mine to avenge; I will repay, says the LORD.

²⁰So if your enemy is hungry, feed him; and if he suffers thirst, then give him something to drink. In doing so, you will be giving him hot coals to carry upon his head. ²¹And be not overtaken with evil but overtake evil with good.

---

1. I am appealing to you because of God's mercy in your lives...

Paul begins this section with an appeal for his readers to consider the mercies of God in their own lives. As priests they were to offer themselves to God as those who were now dead, and yet alive, which is likely what Paul intends in Gal. 2:20 when he declares himself crucified with Christ and yet living.

Such is our reasonable worship.

Cf. "our spiritual worship" (ESV), "the worship offered by mind and heart." (NEB)

2. Do not conform yourselves to the world around you...

Though we live in the present world, we do not conform ourselves to its patterns, or the ever-changing current of the popular culture. For Calvin, the "world around us" signified the sentiments and morals of men, to which we were no longer to conform ourselves.

Be transformed by the renewing of your minds, working out the will of God...

The verb "transform" appears in Matt. 17:1–2 and Mark 9:2 as a referent for the Lord's transfiguration on the mount, and again in 2 Cor. 3:18 as a referent for the transformation of the believers.

> And the Lord—who is the Spirit—makes us more and more like him as we are changed into his glorious image. (NLT)

3. I speak through the grace given to me by God...

Augustine held that while Paul experienced the same grace in his life as other believers, the "grace of apostleship" was the particular grace bestowed on those called to this office.

Be sober-minded, regarding yourselves after the measure of faith given to each of you.

The expression "measure of faith" refers to the efficacy given to each believer for the discharge of their responsibilities in the church, cf. "But to each one of us grace was given according to the measure of Christ's gift" (Eph. 4:7, NASB).

5. We too, having many limbs with different functions, are each joined to the other as one body in Christ.

Paul is the only New Testament writer to use the body as a metaphor for the people of God. The diversity of Christ's body was nowhere more evident than in Rome, where people of diverse cultures, social status, and backgrounds were called to fellowship at one table.

> All of you together are his body and each of you are a part of it. (1 Cor. 12:27)

6. And having our unique gifts, we each serve according to the grace given to us.

What the church calls gifts (charismata) are really manifestations of grace (charis). Paul's list of gifts in chapter 12 (prophecy, teaching, exhorting, etc.) is not exhaustive, but illustrative. By prophecy, he likely means the spirit-led communication of those who edify, exhort, and comfort others in the church (cf. 1 Cor. 14:3; 31).

8. But each according to the faith they have received from God.

Paul lists three attitudes which those who exercise spiritual gifts in the church were to have: (1) Singleness of mind denotes the simplicity of purpose which followers of Christ were to have. (2) Diligence describes the swiftness and enthusiasm of those who serve. And (3) gladness infers the cheerful readiness and willing spirit of believers.

9. Love must be unfeigned.

Paul begins this next section of writing with thirteen exhortations ranging from love and charity to hospitality.

That love must be unfeigned literally means that it should be exercised without hypocrisy, hidden agendas, or selfish motives.

10. Love one another as family.

Paul's redefining of boundaries included an emphasis on family belongingness within the church. One which transcended the usual cultural or ethnic categories in the ancient world. In Christ, those who were once considered to be different or strange, were now seen as family.

11. Do not be lazy in serving the Lord but be lit with the spirit.

Paul may be suggesting a kind of fervency in the Holy Spirit or fervency in the sense of one's own enthusiasm. The same wording is used to describe Apollos in Acts 18:25, cf. "and being fervent in spirit, he spoke and taught accurately the things of the Lord" (KJV).

14. Speak blessings on those who persecute you.

The wording here literally means to speak well to those who persecute you. The same verb, however, is used by Luke in his gospel for blessing, cf. "Bless those who curse you" (Lk. 6:28, NLT).

15. Rejoice with those who rejoice and mourn with those who mourn.

Paul's readers were to share in both the joy and mourning of others in the church, and to do good to all people, but especially to those belonging to the family of faith (cf. Gal. 6:10).

16. Be like minded with one another.

Paul reminds his readers that there can be no air of superiority among those who have been made equally dependent upon grace.

17. Do not return evil to others but take thought to what is right and just.

The principle of non-retaliation runs throughout the New Testament but is probably clearest in the Lord's prayer from the Cross: "Father, forgive them, for they don't know what they are doing." (Lk. 23:33–34, NLT).

The particular challenge in reading Paul is not in understanding his instructions, but in practicing them in our own lives.

18. If it is possible—as much as it is in your power—live peaceably with all people.

Paul gives two qualifiers here for living peaceably with others: (1) It must be a possibility (sometimes it's not), and (2) it must be within your power (sometimes it's not).

19. Beloved, do not avenge yourselves against one another, but give place to God's wrath.

Faced with hostility, Christians were not to retaliate against their opponents, but to make room in every situation for God's justice to unfold according to his will (cf. Prov. 20:22; 24:29; Ps. 94:1; Heb. 10:30).

20. So if your enemy is hungry, feed him; and if he suffers thirst, then give him something to drink. In doing so, you will be giving him hot coals to carry upon his head.

Paul here draws from Proverbs 25:21–22. While hot coals may suggest God's judgment on the unrepentant, it is clear from Paul's context that hot coals upon the head of one's enemy is meant to produce benefit or good in their life and not evil

The Bible Knowledge Commentary states the following:

> Sometimes a person's fire went out and he needed to borrow some live coals to restart his fire. Giving a person coals in a pan to carry home "on his head" was a neighborly, kind act; it made friends, not enemies. Also the kindness shown in giving someone food and water makes him ashamed of being an enemy, and brings God's blessing on the benefactor. Compassion, not revenge, should characterize believers...

21. And be not overtaken with evil but overtake evil with good.

While being overtaken with evil means adopting evil itself as one's response to conflict or difficulty, overtaking evil with good means rendering blessing or good to the ones who have offended you.

XIV

FAITH AND GOVERNMENT

Romans 13:1–14

13 Let everyone be subject to the civil authorities, knowing that such authorities are established by God and exist by his will. ² Those who strive against them are striving against the ordinances of God and bring judgment upon themselves.

³ For civil authorities are not a threat for anyone who does well, but only to those who do wrong. If you wish to live without fear of civil powers then do well, and they will honor you, ⁴ for they are God's servants and established for your good. But if you do wrong then you are right to fear, for they have the power to exact punishment as God's servants sent to execute judgment on those who do wrong. ⁵ It is necessary then, that we obey the civil authorities. Not just to avoid punishment, but for the sake of our own conscience.

⁶ For this reason, we also pay taxes, for those bearing authority are God's servants, attending to these matters continually. ⁷ Therefore render to each what is due: taxes to whom taxes, revenue to whom revenue, reverence to whom reverence, and honor to whom honor.

⁸ Owe no one anything except to love them: for the one who loves has fulfilled the law. ⁹ For all the commandments regarding adultery, killing, theft, false witness, coveting, and all other such things, are all summed up in the command to love your neighbor as yourself. ¹⁰ For love does no wrong to another, and in this way, it fulfills the law.

¹¹ Now we know that time is passing, and the hour to awaken has come. Our deliverance is nearer than when we first came to faith. ¹² The night is spent, and the day is upon us. Let us therefore put aside the works of darkness and take

up the armor of light; [13] walking in decency as in the day, and not reveling in drunkenness nor sexual perversion, nor in fighting or jealousy. [14] Let us instead take upon ourselves the Lord Jesus Christ and make no more allowance for the flesh or its desires.

Unlike national Israel, the church was never organized as a state or civil government or intended to replace the ancient world's secular powers. In writing to Rome, it was important that Paul clarify the extent of the believer's duty toward civil authorities and earthly powers, and the boundary markers of their citizenship in this world.

1. Let everyone be subject to the civil authorities...

The civil authorities referred to by Paul belonged to Rome and governed the secular life of people throughout the empire.

Such authorities are established by God and exist by his will.

Regarding the exercise of his secular authority, Jesus says to Pilate:

> You would have no authority over me, if it were not given to you from above. (Jn. 19:11)

Daniel too says of earthly kingdoms and governments:

> The Most High is sovereign over the kingdoms of earth and gives them to whoever he wills. (Dan. 4:17)

2. Those who strive against them are striving against the ordinances of God and bring judgment upon themselves.

While Paul teaches that opposing established governments may be tantamount to opposing God, Sailhamer suggests that Paul is here referring to governments in the ideal sense, meaning those who maintain good and not evil within human societies (1994, p. 531).

It was possible in rare cases that one's faith might necessitate active disobedience to civil powers, as when those powers demand that which is contrary to conscience and faith. This has been the accepted position within the church since the time of the apostles, who openly declared "we must obey God rather than men" (Acts 5:29, NASB).

It should also be noted that while secular or civil governments are honored by the church, they are not given any standing within the body of Christ itself, or in matters of Christian polity or faith (cf. 1 Cor. 6:4).

3. Civil authorities are not a threat for anyone who does well…

The question of unjust secular authorities arose for the church in Rome in AD 64, not long after Paul dictated his letter. When a fire set in the capital destroyed nearly three quarters of the city, Nero blamed Christians for the fire, and believers were eventually rounded up and put to death in large numbers. The historian Tacitus wrote:

> In their very deaths they were made the subjects of sport: for they were covered with the hides of wild beasts, and worried to death by dogs, or nailed to crosses, or set fire to… (Tacitus)

Paul does not address the question of unjust secular authority head on in his letter, presumably because the question itself had not yet arisen.

4. They are God's servants and established for your good.

Paul taught that civil rulers, whether believers or unbelievers, were also God's agents for our good. God himself refers to Nebuchadnezzar of Babylon as his servant (Jer. 25:9), and calls Cyrus of Persia his anointed one, or "messiah" (Isa. 45:1).

They have the power to exact punishment as God's servants sent to execute judgment on those who do wrong.

Cf. "he does not bear the sword in vain" (ESV). The sword was the most visible symbol of the Roman magistrate's military and judicial authority, and his right to punish wrongdoers on behalf of the state.

5. For the sake of our own conscience.

Though he mentions the sword of the magistrate, Paul notes that a higher motive for complying with secular powers is maintaining a good conscience before God.

6. For this reason, we also pay taxes, for those bearing authority are God's servants, attending to these matters continually.

When Paul says that we also pay taxes, his words are either a statement of fact ("for this reason you have been paying taxes") or an imperative ("from now on pay your taxes"). Either way, he is arguing that the civil worker is a servant for our benefit, and deserving of the wage they likely receive through our payment of taxes.

7. Render to each what is due.

Paul may here have in mind an echo of the Lord's command to render unto Caesar what is Caesar's. He elsewhere urges the believer to offer prayers and intercession for those in authority, that they themselves might live peaceful and quiet lives before God (1 Tim. 2:1–2).

8. The one who loves has fulfilled the law.

It is the obligation of believers to seek the welfare of others. The love enjoined upon them is charitable, self-sacrificing, and benevolent by nature and definition.

9. Adultery, killing, theft, false witness, coveting...

Paul here cites the seventh, sixth, eighth, ninth and tenth commandments (cf. Ex. 20:13–17; Dt. 5:17–21), concluding with the admonition to love one's neighbor (Lev. 19:18), which Jesus called the "second great commandment" (Matt. 22:39; Mk. 12:31).

10. Love does no wrong to another, and in this way, it fulfills the law.

The fulfillment of the Law may imply fulfilling its intent. This is perhaps the meaning implied by Jesus when he says, "I have not come to abolish [the Law and the Prophets], but to fulfill them" (Matt. 5:17).

12. Let us therefore put aside the works of darkness and take up the armor of light.

The darkness of the world is here contrasted with the light taken up through faith and the work of the Spirit. Paul frequently characterizes light as a type of armor worn by believers who are actively at war with principalities, dark powers, and spiritual wickedness (cf. Eph. 6:12).

14. Let us instead take upon ourselves the Lord Jesus Christ.

Cf. "clothe yourselves with the Lord Jesus Christ" (BSB); "put on the Lord Jesus" (NASB).

An interesting parallel to Paul's use of the verb *endusasthe* (to clothe or be clothed with) is found in the Roman Antiquities of Dionysius, where to "put on Tarquin" meant to "play the part of Tarquin" (11.5). In this sense, putting on Christ would mean taking upon ourselves the life and spirit of Jesus himself, and being clothed in his righteousness.

It should also be noted that taking upon ourselves the image of the risen Son,[50] is the only adornment of the soul (the inner man) that Paul allows in his writings.

---

[50] *"We shall also bear the image of the man of heaven"* (1 Cor. 15:49); see also, 1 Cor. 3:18

XV

LIBERTY AND CONSCIENCE

Romans 14:1–23

14 Receive those who are weaker than you in faith, but not to argue over difficult points. ² For one person believes that all foods are lawful to eat: while another who is weaker in faith believes they can only eat vegetables. ³ The one who eats should not look down on the one who doesn't, and the one who doesn't, should not condemn the one who does—for God has received him.

⁴ Who are you to judge someone else's servant? They will either stand or fall before their own master. And surely, they will stand, because their Master is able to make them stand.

⁵ In the same way, one person believes that one day is more holy than another: yet another sees every day as being the same. Let each be persuaded in their own mind. ⁶ He that observes the day as holy, observes it before the Lord; and he that does not observe it, does not observe it, but is still before the Lord. In the same manner, he that eats, eats before the Lord, and gives thanks unto God; and he that abstains, abstains before the Lord, but he too gives thanks.

⁷ You see that no one lives or dies to themselves. ⁸ If we live, we live unto the Lord; and if we die, we die unto the Lord: so, whether we live or die, it is unto the Lord. ⁹ For this reason Christ died and rose, that he might be Lord over both the dead and the living.

¹⁰ So why are you still condemning one another? For what reason do you despise your brother? For we shall each stand before the judgment seat of God for ourselves, ¹¹ even as it is written:

> As I live, says the LORD, every knee shall bow before me, and
> every tongue shall confess unto God.

[12] Each of us must therefore give an accounting of ourselves before God. [13] So let us not judge one another. If we desire to exercise our judgement, then let us judge ourselves, and stop placing stumbling blocks and snares in front of our brothers.

[14] I know, and am persuaded in the Lord Jesus, that nothing is unclean of itself, but becomes unclean for anyone who regards it as such. [15] But if your brother becomes grieved by what you're eating, then are you still walking in love when you eat? Don't let something like food tear down someone for whom Christ died, [16] or allow what you consider good to make others blaspheme.

[17] God's kingdom is not a matter of food and drink, but of justice and peace, and joy in the Holy Spirit. [18] Anyone serving Christ in this way pleases God and is approved of men. [19] Let us therefore establish peace and build one another up. [20] Don't pull down God's work because of food! All things are pure; but they become evil if they cause someone else to stumble. [21] It is better to avoid meats and wine, and anything else if it causes someone else to stumble or sin.

[22] Hold your faith firmly between you and God. If you have decided a thing is right and act without passing judgment on yourself, then you are blessed. [23] But if you act while in doubt then you are condemning yourself already, even in something like eating, because what you are doing is not being done in faith. And whatever is not of faith is sin.

As Jewish and non-Jewish Christians entered into fellowship it was natural for conflicts to arise between them. In fact, such conflicts were inevitable as the differing cultures and social norms came into tension.

While ethnic and cultural norms were embedded in Jewish religion from the beginning, non-Jewish members of the church failed to see anything wrong with eating meats sold in pagan temples, drinking wine, or not honoring certain days of the week over others.

Paul's message to the church on these matters can be summed up as follows: Unity does not require agreement on every point, and acceptance of others should also allow plenty of room for differences.

1. Receive those who are weaker than you in faith, but not to argue over difficult points.

Paul begins by stressing the importance of receiving one another, but not for the sake of quarreling over matters such as worship or diet. The weaker in faith were likely those who did not accept all foods as being equally kosher ("fit"), or all days as being equally holy.

2. For one person believes that all foods are lawful to eat: while another who is weaker in faith believes they can only eat vegetables.

While those who were stronger in their faith understood that their diet did not determine their standing with God, those who were weaker in this area avoided eating meats sacrificed in pagan temples. It should be remembered that eating itself is neither good nor bad, and that believers have not been forbidden from eating anything on moral grounds alone (cf. 1 Tim. 4:3–4).

> It's true that we can't win God's approval by what we eat. We don't lose anything if we don't eat it, and we don't gain anything if we do. (1 Cor. 8:8, NLT).

3. For God has received him.

God's action in receiving both the strong and the weak is the same action which Paul elsewhere asks his readers to take with one another, cf. "receive one another, even as Christ has received you" (15:7). In doing so, he neither derides the weak for their weakness, nor commends the strong for their strength. His primary concern is the unity of the church and not encouraging airs of superiority amongst its members.

4. Who are you to judge someone else's servant? They will either stand or fall before their own master.

Paul challenges those in the church who felt they had a right to judge other believers in debatable matters, reminding them that the right to judge Christ's servants belonged to none other than Christ himself.

5. Let each be persuaded in their own mind.

Cf. "Don't let anyone condemn you for what you eat or drink, or for not celebrating certain holy days or new moon ceremonies or Sabbaths" (Col. 2:16, NLT).

6. He that observes the day as holy, observes it before the Lord.

Many Jewish believers observed the Sabbath and other Jewish feast-days because they were a part of their cultural heritage, while Gentile believers had no such heritage to draw from. Paul insists they were not to be judged for failing to observe the same days observed by Jews.

> You are trying to earn favor with God by observing certain days or months or seasons or years. I fear for you. (Gal. 4:10–11, NLT)

Paul's point is that each person must be fully persuaded in their own mind that they are doing the right things before God.

He that eats, eats before the Lord, and gives thanks unto God.

> Cf. Why is my freedom being judged by another's conscience? If I have partaken with thankfulness, then why am I being slandered for that which I gave thanks? (1 Cor. 10:29–30)

9. That he might be Lord over both the dead and the living.

Jesus alone is Lord over the dead and the living. What this means for Paul is that Christ alone is the rightful Judge of his servants, and not we.

10. So why are you still condemning one another?

Because Christ is the only true judge, believers were not to judge one another in questionable areas of conduct; for Christ himself will judge each soul according to his own standard.

If we insist on passing swift, uninformed, and unloving judgment on our brothers, then we have forgotten that in reviling them we are also reviling the Lord whose name they bear.

For we shall each stand before the judgment seat of God for ourselves.

The judgment seat of God, also referred to as the judgment seat of Christ, is the tribunal where believers will receive their recompense for things done in the body (cf. 2 Cor. 5:10).

11. As I live, says the LORD, every knee shall bow before me, and every tongue shall confess unto God.

Quoted from Isaiah 45:23, both here and in Philippians 2. In both cases the claim that Paul is making for Christ is the precise claim that Isaiah had made for Yahweh:

> Turn to Me and be saved all you ends of the earth, for I am God, and there is no other. I have sworn by Myself, and the word has gone forth from My mouth in righteousness and will not return, that unto Me every knee shall bow, and every tongue shall confess, saying "in the LORD alone is there righteousness and strength. (Isa. 45:22-24)

12. Each of us must therefore give an accounting of ourselves before God.

It is not for the souls of others that we will give an answer to God, but for the soul of ourselves. To this accounting we shall bring nothing else except our own soul and character.

13. If we desire to exercise our judgement, then let us judge ourselves, and stop placing stumbling blocks and snares in front of our brothers.

A Christian stumbles when they knowingly engage in behaviors that are in conflict with their own conscience. The stumbling block that we are not to place in front of others is the public exercise of our liberties when those liberties are in conflict with things held in the conscience of our neighbors.

> Take care that your liberty does not become a point of stumbling for the weak. (1 Cor. 8:9)

14. I know, and am persuaded in the Lord Jesus, that nothing is unclean of itself, but becomes unclean for anyone who regards it as such.

Cf. "To the pure, all things are pure, but to the defiled and those without faith, nothing is pure" (Titus 1:15). Defilement, Bruce wrote, is found in people's minds, not in the objects and foods they allow themselves.

15. Don't let something like food tear down someone for whom Christ died.

If your behavior creates a problem for another believer, then your behavior—even if it is permissible, is without love, cf. "All things are lawful for me, but not all things are beneficial" (1 Cor. 6:12).

Paul reminds us that we are to consider the welfare of others when deciding upon a course of action, or an indulgence, even if it is permissible, cf. "If what I eat is a snare for my brother, then I will cease eating even meat, that I might not be a snare unto him" (cf. 1 Cor. 8:13).

16. Or allow what you consider good to make others blaspheme.

The good referred to here are the things allowed by one's conscience. These should not be spoken of as evil when it is God himself who has given the individual the liberty to partake in them.

17. God's kingdom is not a matter of food and drink, but of justice and peace, and joy in the Holy Spirit.

By justice, peace and joy in the Holy Spirit, Paul likely intends their visible fruits, i.e., the behaviors by which these qualities are made apparent to others.

19. Let us therefore establish peace and build one another up.

The strong was to build up the weak by foregoing what is permissible; and the weak was to build up the strong by not judging them in the things their conscience had allowed them.

20. Don't pull down God's work because of food!

Again, the word "food" can be substituted for whatever it is that our conscience has allowed us. God's work in and among the church should not be hindered for the sake of our own personal allowance.

History is full of those who have torn down the unity of the body of Christ for the sake of non-essential matters, opinions, and culture.

21. It is better to avoid meats and wine, and anything else if it causes someone else to stumble or sin.

It was Paul's practice to adapt himself to the social and cultural customs of those he ministered to. In the presence of believing Jews he submitted himself to the Law, while in the company of non-Jewish believers he did not.

22. Hold your faith firmly between you and God.

By faith, Paul means one's conviction that their actions are just, and in violation of neither God's will nor one's personal conscience.

If you have decided a thing is right and act without passing judgment on yourself, then you are blessed.

In this sense, it is to the strong that Paul is addressing his words, i.e., the one who acts without incurring the condemnation of personal conscience.

23. But if you act while in doubt then you are condemning yourself already...And whatever is not of faith is sin.

Paul here seems to have in mind the weaker brother, meaning the one who acts while incurring the condemnation of their own conscience. The one who acts while knowing that their actions are lawful is acting from a place of faith, while any action taken against the dictates of one's own conscience is sin.

XVI

UNITY AND DIVERSITY

Romans 15:1–22

15 Let those of us who are strong bear with the sensitivities of the weak and not please ourselves. ² For in serving our neighbors and working for their good, we are building them up.

³ And in Christ we see an example of someone who did this very thing. He did not serve himself but served others. For as it is written, the reproaches of those who reproached you fell on me. ⁴ Now what was written, was written for our learning and benefit, that through patience and the calling of God's word, we might have hope.

⁵ Now may the God of all patience and exhortation bring you to a common mind concerning Christ: ⁶ that you may all with one mind and voice glorify the God and Father of our Lord Jesus, ⁷ and receive one another just as Christ received you, to God's glory. ⁸ For Christ came as a servant among the Jews to show God's faithfulness, and to confirm the promises made to their fathers. ⁹ In doing so, he has now brought the nations to mercy as well, that they too might glorify God, even as it is written: For this, I will praise you among the nations; I will sing praises to your name.

¹⁰ Again it says, Rejoice, O nations, with his people. ¹¹ And, Praise the LORD, every nation; and let all the people sing his praise. ¹² And finally, Isaiah says: In that day, the root of Jesse shall arise and reign over the nations. And every nation will place their hope in him.

¹³ May the God of hope now fill you with the joy and peace of your faith, that you too may abound in this hope through the power of the Holy Spirit.

[14] Now brothers, I am thoroughly convinced of the goodness and knowledge that is among you, and that you are well able to exhort one another. [15] Still, I have written more boldly on some points as a reminder to you. For through the grace given to me [16] as Christ's servant to the nations in the gospel, the offering of the nations is being made acceptable to God, and set apart in the Holy Spirit.

[17] I have therefore gloried in Christ concerning the things of God. [18] Yet only in those things which Christ has done through me, in bringing the nations to the obedience of word and deed, [19] in the power of signs and wonders, and in the Spirit. For I have proclaimed the gospel of Christ from Jerusalem and the surrounding regions, all the way to Illyricum. [20] And I have been zealous in proclaiming the gospel, though not in the places where Christ had already been named, so as not to build on the foundation of others. [21] For as it is written:

> They will see, who were not spoken to, and they will understand,
> who had not heard.

[22] And for this reason I have been delayed in visiting you in person.

---

1. Let those of us who are strong bear with the sensitivities of the weak and not please ourselves.

cf. "Those of us who are strong must accept as our own burden the tender scruples of the weak" (REV).

Paul admonishes his stronger readers that they were to bear with the infirmities of the weak, and not seek their own interests. Rather, they were to seek the good of others, and to build them up as God enabled them.

2. For in serving our neighbors and working for their good, we are building them up.

The intent behind our actions should always be the upliftment of others, especially those who belong to the household of faith (Gal. 6:10). By building them up, Paul means that we are contributing to the promotion of their spiritual growth and benefit.

3. For as it is written, the reproaches of those who reproached you fell on me.

Paul uses Psalm 69:9 to show how zeal for the things of God can sometimes lead to insult and reproach from men. Christian faithfulness may sometimes mean bearing insult or even mockery for the sake of others.

4. Now what was written, was written for our learning and benefit, that through patience and the calling of God's word, we might have hope.

Cf. "Now these things happened to them as an example, and they were written for our instruction" (1Cor. 10:11, NASB). The real object of the present verse is to remind us that the things written down in Scripture are written for our learning.

5. Now may the God of all patience and exhortation bring you to a common mind concerning Christ.

Being brought to a common mind doesn't mean agreeing on every point of doctrine or opinion. Paul has already dealt with the need to receive those with whom we may disagree. Rather, he is encouraging his readers to embrace the mind or attitude of Christ toward one another, cf. "As I have loved you, so you must love one another." (Jn. 13:34).

6. That you may all with one mind and voice glorify the God and Father of our Lord Jesus.

Paul wasn't content with members of the church simply tolerating each other's differences. Rather, he insists on the need of a mutual acceptance expressed in the unified worship of the church.

It is the unity expressed in this common worship ("with one mind and voice") that Paul held as the real evidence of unity within the church itself.

7. And receive one another just as Christ received you, to God's glory.

The words "one another" infer the presence of those in the church that differed from one another in some recognizable way, e.g., culture, race, class, etc. Such divisions likely existed between the strong and the weak, ethnic Jews and Gentiles, citizens and slaves, wealthy and poor factions in the church, etc.

8. For Christ came as a servant among the Jews to show God's faithfulness, and to confirm the promises made to their fathers.

It is a peculiar fact of the gospels that Jesus, in his earthly ministry, presented himself almost exclusively to Israel, testifying that he was sent only to the "lost sheep" of that nation alone (Matt. 15:24).

Paul explains that through his exclusive ministry to Israel, Jesus was confirming God's faithfulness to them in sending their Messiah, as well as his fidelity to his covenant promises, cf. "to confirm the promises made unto the fathers" (KJV), "to show that God is faithful" (GNT); "By making good God's promises" (NEB).

9. In doing so, he has now brought the nations to mercy as well...

Paul considered his own life and ministry a medium through which God was fulfilling his promise to create a single covenant-family in Christ; a family made up of not only Jews, but all families of the earth. It was through the gospel, Paul argued, that God was fulfilling this promise. Firstly, to Israel, and secondly, through Israel to the nations.

For this, I will praise you among the nations...

These words express David's rejoicing over the nations that were being added to his kingdom, which was God's heritage. They first appear in 2 Sam. 22:50 and are repeated in Psa. 18:49.

10. Rejoice, O nations, with his people.

This quotation from Deuteronomy 32:43, shows Moses commanding the Gentile nations of his day to shout and rejoice with God's people. Paul likely includes these passages as an encouragement to Jewish Christians to rejoice over their Gentile brothers who were now being called to faith in Israel's God.

11. Praise the LORD, every nation; and let all the people sing his praise.

Quoted from Psalm 117:1, where every nation and people are called to praise the covenant God worshiped by Israel.

12. And every nation will place their hope in him.

Quoted from Isaiah where it is prophesied that the root of Jesse will arise as a sign for not only Israel, but for the other nations as well (Isa. 11:1).

Paul seems to be reminding his Jewish readers that Gentiles were not obligated to come to God by way of Judaism, nor were they being asked by God to embrace the culture of their Jewish brothers, who likely maintained their distinct cultural practices, even after entering into fellowship with the Gentiles.

13. That you too may abound in this hope through the power of the Holy Spirit.

Paul now prays that God will fill his readers with joy and peace, which are the marks of our faith in God.

14. Now brothers, I am thoroughly convinced of the goodness and knowledge that is among you, and that you are well able to exhort one another.

Paul had not written to the church because he believed they were incapable of teaching one another. They were, in his view, already filled with knowledge and able to exhort (admonish, counsel) one another on most matters.

15. I have written more boldly on some points as a reminder to you.

Refreshing the minds of believers was a central feature of the apostles' ministry.

> I will always remind you about these things – even though you already know them and are standing firm in the truth.
> (2 Pet. 1:12, NLT)

Through the grace given to me.

Paul states that it was God's grace in him that made him write bolder on some points. He had not planted the church in Rome, nor had he visited them in the past. As an apostle to the nations, however, he likely felt an affinity for Rome's largely Gentile congregation and may have harbored some sense of responsibility for the church in that city.

16. As Christ's servant to the nations in the gospel...

The word translated as servant was mostly used of Temple workers and may reflect Paul's conviction that his apostolate was priestly in nature.

And set apart in the Holy Spirit.

Many Jewish believers considered Gentile Christians to be unclean if they had not been formally converted as Jews. Paul points out that it is the Spirit of God alone that makes men acceptable and holy in God's sight, and not the works added to their faith after (cf. Acts 15:8–9).

18. In bringing the nations to the obedience of word and deed...

Obedience of word and deed may imply coming to faith in Jesus and then following our faith with action, which Paul elsewhere refers to as the obedience of faith (cf. Rom. 1:5).

19. In the power of signs and wonders, and in the Spirit.

While signs are the peculiar graces that point us beyond ourselves to something greater, wonders are physical things (or events) which leave a spiritual imprint on their witness. The power behind both is the Spirit of God.

For I have proclaimed the gospel of Christ from Jerusalem and the surrounding regions, all the way to Illyricum.

While Jerusalem would have marked the southeastern limits covered by Paul in his ministry, Illyricum, which joined the northern border of Macedonia, would have marked the northwestern limits. Together, the words Jerusalem to Illyricum defined the geographical limits of Paul's ministry thus far, which was roughly a distance of 1,400 miles.

20. So as not to build on the foundation of others.

Paul famously established churches in places where Jesus had not yet been named. As an apostle, he laid a foundation upon which others built, though not always to his liking, cf. "Let each one take care how he builds upon it" (1 Cor. 3:10, ESV).

21. They will see, of whom he was not spoken, and they will understand, who had not heard.

Isaiah 52:15, quoted from the LXX, is a referent to the many nations and kings who will one day come to faith through the Servant of the LORD.

22. For this reason I have been delayed in visiting you in person.

Paul concludes by emphasizing that his labors from Jerusalem to Illyricum are the reason for his delay in visiting Rome, cf. "My visit to you has been delayed so long because I have been preaching in these places" (15:22, NLT).

GREETINGS AND COMMENDATIONS

Romans 15:23–16:27

²³ But now, having no place left to minister in these parts, I will see you at last, as has been my desire. ²⁴ As I make my way into Spain, I am hoping to be equipped by you as well. After spending some time with you, of course, and being filled by your company.

²⁵ But first I am heading to Jerusalem to render a service to God's people there. ²⁶ For Macedonia and Achaia thought it well to partner with the poor among the Lord's people in Jerusalem. ²⁷ They were eager to do this; and were in some ways indebted to them. For if other nations have partaken of them spiritually, then it is only right that they minister to them materially. ²⁸ When I have completed this, and given to them this fruit, I will set off by Rome into Spain. ²⁹ And I know that when I come, I will come in the full blessing of Christ.

³⁰ Now I urge you, brothers, through our Lord Jesus Christ, and through the love of the Spirit, that you pray to God on my behalf; ³¹ that I may be delivered from those in Judaea who have not believed; and that my service for Jerusalem would be accepted by God's people there, ³² and that finally, I might come to you in joy and God's will, and be refreshed among you. ³³ May the God of peace be with you all. Amen.

16 May I commend to you our sister Phoebe, who is a deacon of the church at Cenchrea. ² Receive her in the Lord, as is worthy of God's people, and assist her in whatever matters she may have need of you: for she has been a benefactor of many—including me.

[3] Greet Prisca and Aquila also, my fellow laborers in Christ, Jesus, [4] who put their lives at risk for my own: and to whom not only I, but all the Gentile churches are indebted. [5] Send greetings to the church in their house.

Greet Epaenetus, who has been dear to me; and was the first fruits of Christ's harvest in Asia. [6] Greet Mary, who labored on our behalf. [7] Salute Andronicus and Junia, my kinsmen and fellow prisoners, who are well known among the apostles, and who were in Christ even before me. [8] Greet Ampliatus, whom I love in the Lord. [9] Greet Urbane, our fellow worker in Christ, and Stachys, who is dear to me. [10] Greet Apelles, who has proven himself in Christ as well, and greet those in the house of Aristobulus.

[11] Greet my kinsman, Herodion; and those in the house of Narcissus, who are in the Lord. [12] Greet Tryphena and Tryphosa, who have labored in the Lord. Greet Persis, who is well loved, and who has also labored abundantly in the Lord. [13] Greet Rufus, who is chosen in the Lord, and his mother, who is like a mother to me also. [14] Greet Asyncritus, Phlegon, Hermes, Patrobas, Hermas, and the brothers with them. [15] Greet Philologus and Julia, Nereus, his sister, and Olympas, and God's people who are with them. [16] Greet one another with a holy kiss. All the churches of Christ send you greetings.

[17] Now I urge you to mark those who cause divisions among you and bring offenses contrary to the teachings you received. Turn away from them, [18] for they do not serve Christ, our Lord, but their own bellies, and have deceived the unknowing through smooth words and flattery. [19] But your obedience is known in every place, and for that I rejoice over you. But I want you to be wise in the things that are good, and simple in the things that are evil. [20] For the God of peace will soon crush the satan underneath your feet. May the grace of our Lord Jesus be with you all. Amen.

[21] Timothy, my fellow laborer, sends you greetings, as do Lucius, Jason, and Sosipater, my kinsmen. [22] I, Tertius, who set this epistle in writing, greet you in the Lord. [23] Gaius, my host, and the church here, greet you as well. Erastus, the city treasurer, sends greetings also, as does Quartus, another of our brothers. [24] May the grace of our Lord Jesus Christ, be with you all. Amen.

[25] Now to the one who is able to strengthen you according to my gospel—which is the proclamation of Jesus Christ, and the unveiling of the mystery hidden

throughout the ages, [26] but now revealed through the prophets by the decree of the eternal God, to whom every nation is called to the obedience of faith—[27] to God alone, who has all wisdom, and through Jesus alone, who is the Christ, glory to the coming ages!

Amen.

———————— ✦✦✦✦✦✦✦ ————————

23. But now, having no place left to minister in these parts, I will see you at last, as has been my desire.

Paul wants to remind his readers that his desire to see them was not a new one.

24. As I make my way into Spain, I am hoping to be equipped by you as well.

Having spent years ministering in the eastern regions of the empire, Paul now looked to minister in the west, namely Spain. To be equipped meant to be sent forward, provided for, and financially assisted as he advanced into Spain.

25. But first I am heading to Jerusalem to render a service to God's people there.

By organizing a collection for Jerusalem Paul hoped to provide aid for the poorer saints in the city, cement relations between the early church and the Gentile churches he had planted, and remind his Gentile converts, through their giving, of their indebtedness to Jerusalem

27. They were eager to do this; and were in some ways indebted to them.

The indebtedness of the Gentiles stems from the fact that the spiritual things they benefited from had come to them by way of Jerusalem. This indebtedness was not legal, but moral. In writing to the churches, Paul insists that it is an act of grace by which they now give, and not a binding obligation, cf. "see that you excel in this act of grace also" (2 Cor. 8:7, ESV).

28. When I have completed this, and given to them this fruit, I will set off by Rome into Spain.

The offering to Jerusalem was to be a token of the fruit produced by Paul's Gentile mission, as well as a sign of the affection that Gentile believers held for the saints in Jerusalem.

30–32. Pray to God on my behalf; that I may be delivered…that my service would be accepted…that I might come to you in joy.

Paul asks his readers for prayer in three specific matters: Deliverance, acceptance, and arrival. He prays for (1) his deliverance from the unbelievers in Judaea, (2) the acceptance of his gift in Jerusalem, (3) and his arrival at Rome in complete joy.

33. May the God of peace be with you all.

Paul ends his request for prayer with a prayer of his own, i.e., that God's presence be with his readers.

Note: The concluding chapter of Romans consists of Paul's extended greetings to members of the church in Rome. Taken as a whole, these names give witness to a diverse mixture of persons, cultures and social classes woven into the single fabric of Rome's burgeoning church.

1. May I commend to you our sister Phoebe, who is a deacon of the church at Cenchrea.

Paul had entrusted Phoebe, a deaconess in the church, with delivering (and perhaps expounding) his letter to the various congregations in Rome. As a personal benefactor of Paul and others, Phoebe would have been a woman of both financial substance and influence.

3. Greet Prisca and Aquila also, my fellow laborers in Christ…

The woman Paul identifies as Prisca is the same woman referred to as Priscilla in Acts (cf. Acts 18:2). It was Prisca and her husband, Aquila, who took the young teacher Apollos under their tutelage in Ephesus, and helped him to better understand the way of God (Acts 18:26).

5. Send greetings to the church in their house.

cf. "the church that meets in their home" (NLT) Meeting for worship and teaching in the homes of believers was the common practice of the early church, as there were no separate church buildings or Christian sanctuaries in the first century.

6. Greet Mary, who labored on our behalf.

Six women in the New Testament bear this name. Paul gives no further clues about the identity of the Mary that he mentions, other than to state that she labored a great deal on behalf of the church.

7. Andronicus and Junia...who are well known among the apostles, and who were in Christ even before me.

This couple were likely Jewish by birth. Paul calls them his kinsmen, and states that they were in Christ before him, and well known among the apostles.

8. Ampliatus, whom I love in the Lord.

This name was common among members of the imperial household, and may refer to a member of the ruling class in Rome.

9. Urbane, our fellow worker in Christ.

The name Urbanós is of Latin origin, and means "belonging to the urbs" or "of the city."

11. My kinsman, Herodion.

By kinsman, Paul may simply mean that Herodian was of Jewish birth.

12. Tryphena and Tryphosa, who have labored in the Lord.

These two women were likely relatives. Both of their names derive from the Greek word "truphē," which can mean softness, daintiness, or luxuriousness.

13. Greet Rufus, who is chosen in the Lord, and his mother, who is like a mother to me also.

The Rufus referred to by Paul is thought by many to have been the son of Simon of Cyrene, the man who bore the cross of Jesus on the way to Golgotha, cf. "a man from Cyrene, named Simon, who is the father of Alexander and Rufus" (Mk. 15:21).

Mark, who is thought to have written for the benefit of believers in Rome, implies that there was a Rufus of some repute dwelling in that city during the time of his writing, and that this Rufus was the son of Simon, who had borne the cross of Jesus. Mark's readers apparently knew Alexander and Rufus well, because he specifically refers to them in order to identify their father.

It is worth noting that when Barnabas brings Paul to Antioch (Acts 11:25–26), there is among the prophets and teachers there a man named Simeon, also called Níger, meaning *dark-skinned* (cf. Acts 13:1), with whom many have identified Simon the father of Rufus. If Simeon and Simon are indeed the same person, then this would have put Paul in contact with Rufus' mother in Antioch as well.

14–15. Paul here names 9 others specifically: *Asyncritus, Phlegon, Hermes, Patrobas, Hermas, Philologus, Julia* (her name implies some association with the imperial household), *Nereus,* and *Olympas* (an abbreviated form of *Olympiodorus*). Very little can be said about these names with any certainty.

16. Greet one another with a holy kiss.

Paul frequently mentions this form of affection between believers (cf. 1 Cor. 16:20; 2 Cor. 13:12; 1 Thess. 5:26; see also 1 Peter 5:14). The kiss is called "holy" to distinguish it from worldly or sexual forms of affection between people.

17. Now I urge you to mark those who cause divisions among you...

By divisions, Paul is likely referring to anything that wrongly separates people into factions. In Gal. 5:20 Paul includes "divisions" among the works of the flesh, indicating that the divisions referred to are manmade, carnal, and not of the spirit.

19. But I want you to be wise in the things that are good, and simple in the things that are evil.

The Greek word for "simple" literally means not mingled or mixed and was sometimes used to describe undiluted wine. Paul desired his readers to remain unmingled or mixed with anything that might corrupt or turn them from the gospel, cf. "a little leaven leavens the whole lump" (Gal. 5:9, NKJV).

20. For the God of peace will soon crush the satan underneath your feet.

There is an obvious echo here of Genesis 3:15, where the woman is assured that her seed will one day bruise the head of the serpent. Though this promise points directly to Jesus, the people of Christ are those who now share in his victory as well.

21. Timothy, my fellow laborer...Lucius, Jason, and Sosipater, my kinsmen.

Paul now mentions four of those with him in Corinth at the time of his writing. Timothy was a native of Lystra, whom Paul regarded as his own son in the faith (cf. Acts 16:1–3; 1 Tim. 1:2; Phil. 2:22). Little is known with certainty about Lucius, Jason, and Sosipater, other than the fact that Paul refers to them as his "kinsmen."

22. I, Tertius, who set this epistle in writing.

Paul may have regularly used an amanuensis (secretary), but Tertius is the only one whose name appears in the body of an actual epistle.

23. Gaius, my host...

The Gaius spoken of here may be the same Gaius that is baptized by Paul in Corinth (1 Cor. 1:14).

25. Now to the one who is able to strengthen you according to my gospel— which is the proclamation of Jesus Christ...

The phrase *euangellion mou* literally means "my gospel" (cf. Rom. 2:16), which is Paul's way of saying, "the gospel as I teach it." It is important to remember that the gospel preached by Paul was the same gospel preached by other apostles.

> Remember Jesus Christ, who was descended from David, and was raised from the dead. This is my gospel. (2 Tim. 2:8)

26. The mystery hidden throughout the ages, but now revealed through the prophets...

Part of the mystery revealed in and through the gospel is that of the nations being made heirs with Israel, and members of one body, and sharers in the promises of God fulfilled in Christ.[51]

27. To God alone, who has all wisdom, and through Jesus alone, who is the Christ,

Paul declares throughout Romans that in Jesus there is a dynamic revelation of the God of creation. The Greek adjective *monō* (alone, only) means that Jesus reveals the very God who is alone (one, only) in glory and wisdom.

In Paul's closing doxology (vv. 25–27) the major themes of his letter are condensed into a few powerful lines, and set before his readers in summary fashion. These themes include:

> [1] God's power to save fallen man. [2] The good news of the Messiah – Jesus Christ. [3] The revelation of God's righteousness. [4] The witness of the Hebrew Scriptures. [5] The call of all nations to obey the gospel. And [6] the saving wisdom of God in Christ, to whom belongs all glory.

---

[51] Ephesians 3:6; cf. also Col. 1:26–27

BIBLIOGRAPHY

PRIMARY SOURCES

The Dead Sea Scrolls in English, tr. by Vermes, G. (1962)
Greek NT: Byzantine Majority Text. Pierpont, W. & Robinson, M. (2005)
The Greek Testament. Alford, H. (1884)
Josephus. Antiquities of the Jews. (AD 93 or 94)
The Lexham English Septuagint. Lexham (2019)
Nestle 1904 Greek New Testament. Nestle, E. (1904)
Novum Testamentum Graece. Ed. by Aland, B., Aland, K., et al (1898)

COMMENTARIES

Bruce, F. F., *Romans: An Introduction and Commentary* (1985)
Calvin, J., *Commentaries on the Epistle of Paul the Apostle to the Romans* (1539)
Cranfield, C. E., *A Critical and Exegetical Commentary on the Epistle...* (1998)
Dunn, J. D. G., *Romans. Word Biblical Commentary series* (1988)
Haldane, R., *Exposition of the Epistle to the Romans* (1835)
Henry, M., *Matthew Henry Commentary on the Whole Bible* (1706)
Horton, S., *The Book of Acts* (1981)
Luther, M., *Lectures on Romans* (1515-16)
McGee, J. V., *Reasoning through Romans.* 2 vols. (1976)
Melanchthon, P., *Commentary on Romans,* tr. by Kramer, F. (1992)
Moo, D., *The Epistle to the Romans. New International Commentary* (1996)
Mounce, R., *Romans. The New American Commentary Series* (1995)
Sailhamer, J. H., *NIV Compact Bible Commentary* (1994)
Sanday, W. & Headlam, A. C., *A Critical and Exegetical Commentary on...* (1902)
Seemuth, D. P., *Romans* (2005)
Spurgeon, C.H., *Spurgeon's Verse Expositions of the Bible, Romans 7* (n.d.)
Walvoord, J. & Zuck, R., *The Bible Knowledge Commentary* (1983)
Witmer, J. A., *Romans* in *The Bible Knowledge Commentary: New Testament* (1983)

OTHER STUDIES

Arminium, J., Works of James Arminius, Vol. 2, Grace and Free Will (1560–1609)

Athanasius, Against the Heathen, circa 328 – 335 AD

Augustine, A., De Spiritu et Littera (412)

Augustine, A., The Works of Aurelius Augustine, tr. Clark, T. (1876)

Bachmann, E. T., ed. Martin Luther's Word and Sacrament I (1960)

Bauckham, R., God Crucified: Monotheism and Christology in the NT (1998)

Bauckham, R., Gospel Women: Studies of the Named Women in the Gospels (2002)

Bauckham, R., Paul's Christology of Divine Identity (2016)

Brown, C., "Righteousness" in The New International Dictionary of NT... (1986)

Duffield, G. & Van Cleave, N. M., Foundations of Pentecostal Theology (1983)

Hayford, J., Hayford's Bible Handbook (1995)

Hayford, J., ed. New Spirit-Filled Life® Bible (2002)

Hayford, J., The Beauty of Spiritual Language (1992)

Hays, R. B., The Conversion of the Imagination: Paul as Interpreter of... (2005)

Hays, R. B., Echoes of Scripture in the Letters of Paul (1993)

Heiser, M. S., Paul's Use of Genesis 15:5 in Romans 4:18 in Light of Early Jewish Deification Traditions (2017)

Heiser, M. S., The Unseen Realm: Recovering the Supernatural Worldview... (2015)

Hurtado, L. W., One God, One Lord (1998)

Käsemann, E., Perspectives on Paul (1971)

Lasley, W. F., Paul's Salvation Letters (2002)

Lenski, R. The Interpretation of St. Paul's Epistle to the Romans (1961)

Levin, M., With All Your Heart: The Shema in Jewish Worship (2002)

Luther, M., "Preface to the Epistle to the Romans" (1522), in Works of Martin Luther (1932), Vol. VI

Mackie, T., What is the Shema? (2017) retrieved from bibleproject.com

Menzies, W. & Horton, S. M., Bible Doctrines: A Pentecostal Perspective (1993)

NAS New Testament Greek Lexicon from biblestudytools.com (1999)

Nanos, M. D., Paul and the Jewish Tradition: The Ideology of the Shema (2012)

Ortlund, D., Inaugurated Glorification. Revisiting Romans 8:30 (2014)

Piper, J., Who is a True Jew, Pt. I (1999)

Ryrie, C. C., Basic Theology (1986)

Robertson, A. T., Word Pictures in the New Testament (1931)

Sanders, E. P., Paul and Palestinian Judaism (1977)

Schattenmann, J., κοινωνία, Dictionary of New Testament Theology, 1 (1979)

Scofield, C. I., The New Scofield Reference Bible (1967)

Smith, W., Smith's Bible Dictionary (2004)

Tertullian, On the Resurrection of the Flesh (c. 160–240 A.D.)

Toussaint, S. D., *Suffering in Acts and the Pauline Epistles*, in *Why, O God? Suffering and Disability in the Bible and Church* (2011)

Unger, M. F., "Righteousness" in *The New Unger's Bible Dictionary* (1988)

Vincent, M., *Word Studies in the New Testament* (1900)

Von Rad, G., *Old Testament Theology I* (1962)

Wright, N. T. & Bird, M. F., *The New Testament in Its World* (2019)

Printed in the United States
by Baker & Taylor Publisher Services